LIBRARIES
AND SCHOLARLY
COMMUNICATION
IN THE
UNITED STATES

Also in the Beta Phi Mu Monograph Series

"An Active Instrument for Propaganda": The American Public Library During World War I
Wayne A. Wiegand

LIBRARIES AND SCHOLARLY COMMUNICATION IN THE UNITED STATES

The Historical Dimension

Edited by
Phyllis Dain and John Y. Cole

Beta Phi Mu Monograph, Number 2

GREENWOOD PRESS
New York • Westport, Connecticut • London

Library of Congress Cataloging-in-Publication Data

Libraries and scholarly communication in the United States : the
  historical dimension / edited by Phyllis Dain and John Y. Cole.
    p. cm. — (Beta Phi Mu monograph, ISSN 1041-2751 ; no. 2)
  ISBN 0-313-26807-X (lib. bdg. : alk. paper)
  1. Research libraries—United States—History. 2. Libraries and
scholars—United States—History. 3. Communication and culture—
United States. 4. United States—Intellectual life. I. Dain,
Phyllis. II. Cole, John Young. III. Series.
Z675.R45L53 1990
027.7'0973—dc20   89-23248

British Library Cataloguing in Publication Data is available.

Copyright © 1990 by Beta Phi Mu

All rights reserved. No portion of this book may be
reproduced, by any process or technique, without the
express written consent of the publisher.

Library of Congress Catalog Card Number: 89-23248
ISBN: 0-313-26807-X
ISSN: 1041-2751

First published in 1990

Greenwood Press, Inc.
88 Post Road West, Westport, Connecticut 06881

Printed in the United States of America

The paper used in this book complies with the
Permanent Paper Standard issued by the National
Information Standards Organization (Z39.48-1984).

10 9 8 7 6 5 4 3 2 1

Contents

Acknowledgments vii

Introduction ix

1. Scholarship, Higher Education, and Libraries in the United States: Historical Questions and Quests 1
   Phyllis Dain

2. The Library of Congress and American Scholarship, 1865–1939 45
   John Y. Cole

3. Special Collections and Academic Scholarship: A Tangled Relationship 63
   Neil Harris

4. Research Libraries, the Ideology of Reading, and Scholarly Communication, 1876–1900 71
   Wayne A. Wiegand

5. Preservation, Library Collections, and the Concept of Cultural Property 89
   Paul N. Banks

6. Scholarly Resources for the Study of the Third World: The Case of Africa 111
   Mary Niles Maack

Index 135

About the Contributors 147

Acknowledgments

A number of persons and institutions helped to make possible this book and the conference on "Libraries and Scholarly Communication in the United States: The Historical Dimension."

Dean Robert Wedgeworth of the School of Library Service of Columbia University was closely involved from the beginning in planning the conference and the book. He was personally helpful and supportive and made the resources of the School of Library Service available at all times. The Council on Library Resources awarded a substantial grant toward the expenses of the conference. The Center for the Book in the Library of Congress was generous with its resources; we wish to thank in particular Anne Boni of the center's staff for helping to organize the conference.

We are grateful to Wayne A. Wiegand, editor of the Beta Phi Mu series, for his useful suggestions, and to Loomis Mayer, editor for library and information science at Greenwood Press, and Meg Fergusson, production editor, for guiding us through the publication process.

All the speakers and participants in the 1987 conference contributed to its success, and their comments and conversation have informed the papers included in this volume.

Finally, we wish to thank our spouses, Norman Dain and Nancy Gwinn, for their loving support and critical eyes, with an extra thanks to Nancy Gwinn for writing the fine summary of the conference, as noted in the introduction.

Introduction

Libraries are acknowledged, and prized, as repositories of the records of human activity and communication and as indispensable instruments of cultural and intellectual life. Their existence in history is seen as evidence of high civilization. And we know of past cultures through the materials preserved in our present libraries, which constitute our collective memory. In the modern world, where documentation and communication of knowledge are integral to the creation and affirmation of knowledge, scholarly libraries have been essential to the intellectual process.

In recent years scholarly communication has become a concern of intellectual historians and sociologists who are interested in ideas and intellectual systems and in the social and institutional contexts in which ideas originate and are diffused. In this new intellectual history, little attention has been paid to the role of access to documents and information through the library and through the profession of librarianship, both of which exist to preserve, organize, and disseminate information and knowledge. Librarians, of course, are interested in their role in society, today and in the future. In their effort to adapt to a new world of information technology and information "overload," they are inescapably aware of their historical legacy of buildings, collections, catalogs, methods of operation, and intellectual assumptions. Study of the historical dimension of the role of libraries and librarianship in the scholarly enterprise offers insights into the genesis of current problems and informs our plans for the future. Historians of libraries have created a growing body of useful works, including books and articles that relate library history to the mainstream of social and intellectual history. Many questions remain to be investigated, however. The publication in 1988 by the American Council of Learned Societies of *Writings on Scholarly Communication: An Annotated*

Bibliography of Books and Articles on Publishing, Libraries, Scholarly Research, and Related Issues documents and amplifies the importance of these questions.

The papers in this volume were selected from presentations at an interdisciplinary conference, "Libraries and Scholarly Communication in the United States: The Historical Dimension," which brought library historians and practitioners together with social historians and others concerned with the creation and communication of knowledge. Some seventy participants from various fields met at the Library of Congress on October 29-31, 1987, at the invitation of the School of Library Service of Columbia University and The Center for the Book in the Library of Congress.

The event commemorated two important anniversaries—the hundredth anniversary of the first school for librarians in the United States, founded at Columbia, and the tenth anniversary of the Center for the Book. The school, in its several metamorphoses (culminating in the present School of Library Service at Columbia), has contributed powerfully to modern librarianship through educating generations of library leaders and practitioners. It also has advanced, through the research, publications, and professional work of its faculty and graduates, our understanding of the processes and forms of communicating knowledge and information and their historical, intellectual, and social contexts. The Center for the Book was established in 1977 to promote books and reading and to encourage the interdisciplinary study of books. Through its varied programs and publications, the center stimulates distinguished scholarship in the history of books, libraries, and learning. It also serves as a catalyst in focusing national attention on the importance of books, reading, and the written word.

These mutual interests led to the collaboration of the School of Library Service and the Center for the Book in sponsoring the conference, which was also supported in part by a grant from the Council on Library Resources. Library historians, research librarians, intellectual historians, historians of education, historical bibliographers, representatives of scholarly societies, foundations, and publishers, and other interested persons gathered to hear and discuss recent research and thought on the history of libraries and of scholarly communication. The result was an enthusiastic and exciting series of formal and informal exchanges among all the conference attendees.

The meeting was organized to consider the contributions of libraries and bibliographic enterprises to the processes of scholarly communication; to reexamine the intellectual and cultural assumptions upon which scholarly resources and bibliographic services have developed; and to analyze the scholarly library as a social and cultural institution. The eight research papers, plus commentaries and a keynote address by Patricia Battin, president of the Commission on Preservation and Access, accomplished these goals admirably. The speakers investigated aspects of scholarly communication such as institutional structures and functions; the nature and dissemination of scholarly resources in the humanities, sciences, and social sciences; and concepts of special collections, cultural property, and the uses of knowledge. Several papers focused on the United States; others took the comparative approach or dealt with relationships between the United States and publishing and scholarship abroad, including the Third World. A summary report of the conference, written by Nancy E. Gwinn, Assistant Director of Collections Management at the Smithsonian Institution Libraries, was published in the Library of Congress *Information Bulletin*[1] and as "Libraries and Scholarly Communication in the United States, The Historical Dimension: A Summary," in the quarterly journal *Libraries & Culture*.[2]

The selection of papers published here exemplifies the quality and tenor of the conference and the original research and thought that we, as the organizers and editors, hoped to stimulate. Although varied in approach and scope, the papers are linked by a common interest in probing the nature of scholarly communication and its institutional and material manifestations, and by the view that libraries and librarianship are social creations and social systems. The diversity of the papers and their combination of conceptual and empirical modes point up the complexity and richness of such investigation. Thus these papers, themselves substantial contributions to knowledge, also point the way to future research and discussion on themes of increasing importance to those concerned with scholarship, libraries, and the life of the mind.

NOTES

1. "Report from a Conference at the Library on Libraries and Scholarly Communication in the United States," U.S. Library of Congress *Information Bulletin* 47 (April 18, 1988): 164–167.

2. *Libraries & Culture* 23 (Fall 1988): 499–506.

1

Scholarship, Higher Education, and Libraries in the United States: Historical Questions and Quests

Phyllis Dain

In 1816, a young Bostonian studying in Germany wrote home of his discovery "that the Library is not only the first convenience of a University, but that it is the first necessity,—that it is the life and spirit,—and that all other considerations must yield to the prevalent one of increasing and opening it, and opening it on the most liberal terms to *all* who are disposed to make use of it."[1] George Ticknor was complaining about the lack of such consciousness in America, particularly at Harvard. By the end of the century, American university presidents and other orators seem to have gotten the message: at dedications, cornerstone layings, and other ceremonial occasions libraries were being hailed as the heart of the university. In our culture scarcely anyone would dispute the value of books and reading, or of access to the "word," that libraries signify. Scarcely anyone could conceive of an advanced society without extensive libraries. It is rare to find a book in the humanities and social sciences without acknowledgments to libraries and librarians; and in the less document-based sciences the obligatory reviews of the literature testify to visits to the library. In assessments of academic institutions and graduate programs, rankings of quality have been shown to be highly associated with library facilities,[2] which have also figured in recruiting faculty members and graduate students. Research libraries represent a substantial investment in collections, people, physical plants, and technology. By 1987, the 118 members of the elite Association of Research Libraries (ARL) had altogether well over 300 million volumes, of which the university libraries' share was over 280 million. Operating expenditures totalled more than $1.5 billion and for the university libraries, over one billion. Salaries and wages amounted to nearly $8 million, with a university share of nearly $6 million.[3]

Over the past twenty-five years, we have seen the emergence of scholarly interest in the social, structural, and historical aspects of knowledge and information. Information scientists examine information-seeking behavior and communication among researchers, plus the nature of scholarly and scientific literatures. Sociologists study intellectual, scientific, and cultural authority and the learned professions. Practitioners of a "new" intellectual history have been delving into the social organization and structures of intellectual and academic life, as well as the modes and contexts of creating and disseminating ideas—the historical sociology of knowledge and the emergence of professions. Key to the new history of the book has been interest in the communication of ideas and information, and the new history of science has stimulated people to search for and analyze what Thomas Kuhn has called intellectual paradigms; Derek de Solla Price has shown statistical relationships between scientific publication and scientific development and suggested the importance of the "invisible college"; I. Bernard Cohen has posited the creation of formal communication networks as a necessary stage in modern scientific revolutions.[4]

Libraries—collections of records of human communication, organized for use—have not been mere servants of this world of knowledge, but component parts of it. They can be viewed as information systems that both reflect and influence, and even help to create, paradigms and authority, for they set limits in various ways on the ideas and information available to users. At the same time, if they are big enough and varied enough, they can open boundaries and evoke new ideas or new configurations. The extraordinary magnitude and accessibility of many American libraries allow the curious and the adventurous to poke and pry among the tomes for their own purposes: such libraries invite "chance encounters," the "randomness" of "*creative* research," as one humanist has put it.[5]

Most scholars, if asked, would probably acknowledge that libraries have been essential, even indispensable, to intellectual development. But few scholars are interested in libraries as such. Precisely what place libraries have had in the processes of scholarly communication, the actual and specific connections between libraries and scholarly work, and especially the role of library collections and services in the major intellectual turning points that historians study, is not well known. Librarians and library historians have some understanding of these issues, non-librarians much less so.[6] This can also be said in regard to our contemporary situation. A recent example is a national conference held in March 1987, sponsored by the Columbia University School of Library Service and the University of Colorado, on the role of libraries in the current concern for quality in higher education. The conference proved to be a consciousness-raising experience about libraries for the leading educators and educational administrators in attendance.[7]

In a notable collection of essays on *The Organization of Knowledge in Modern America, 1860–1920,* historian John Higham, in an overview contribution, comments:

> In 1860 there was no American university fully worthy of the name. The United States had no libraries of national or international renown, no industrial laboratories or great private foundations, no widely based learned societies devoted exclusively to the advancement of knowledge within a single limited field. In the late nineteenth and early twentieth centuries all these agencies took shape. Interlocking with one another, they constituted a matrix for research that has survived to this day.[8]

But non-librarians writing on the subject have not as a rule substantially or very seriously considered this matrix in terms of libraries, either as hypothesis or as given phenomenon,[9] although there is considerable library literature to draw upon. The crucial social and intellectual functions of preserving and organizing records of human communication and providing for their use have not attracted even historians, who perhaps most depend upon such records.

In computer parlance, the operation of software without display of the process is called transparency, a desirable feature in electronic library catalogs. Libraries themselves have in a sense always been "transparent." The organizational and intellectual efforts to develop their collections and services are taken for granted; not well understood, these efforts are often unappreciated; and their history is mostly unexplored except by library historians, who are usually librarians and tend to publish in the professional library press. The result is a gap in the delineation by historians of the contexts and institutional structures of American cultural and intellectual life.

The problem is compounded by what Thomas Bender, in his history of intellectual life in New York City, calls the "academicization of knowledge and art in our time."[10] His book can be seen as a response to his own comments ten years ago at the Wingspread Conference on New Directions in American Intellectual History, when he discussed the need to integrate intellectual, social, and especially urban, history. Neither intellectual historians nor urban historians, he said then, have given much attention to the local community, the city, "as a context and audience for intellectual life" and as an environment in which to study the university's domination of that life.[11] This academic hegemony—plus the specialization characterizing contemporary historical research—has meant that much of the work on scholarship, higher learning, and knowledge institutions tends to focus on the university.[12] The result is an imperfect, incomplete understanding of the range and complexity of intellectual life in our time and indeed before our time, when the university was not such a central institution. Among the missing nonacademic components are nonuniversity libraries, particularly public libraries, those general collections for free public use that were founded in the nineteenth century as contributions to civic culture. In his New York City study, Bender allows that "almost as much as libraries, restaurants are central institutions in New York City's intellectual life."[13] While he discusses libraries here and there he neglects to examine them, although serious consideration of their history would contribute to his concepts of community, class, and democracy.

A good deal of research has been done by library historians on the history of public libraries, whose obvious social significance makes them more appealing as subjects than academic libraries, though during the past ten years there has been some interesting work on university libraries. In part because of a somewhat narrow concept of social significance, as well as the phenomenon of "academicization," historical study of public libraries tends, with exceptions, to give insufficient consideration to their role in support of research and advanced study and to their connections with local intellectual life. The rather firm lines within librarianship between institutional types have been perpetuated in much historical writing, where trans-institutional, comparative, or noninstitutional approaches to support of scholarly and educational endeavors are not too common. Historians of education—Bernard Bailyn's and Lawrence Cremin's broad concepts of education notwithstanding—have been, at least in book-length works, preponderantly interested in modes and agencies of formal instruction.[14]

Library resources and services and the library profession are only a part of the complex interplay of forces comprising intellectual life, but a part whose value we need to know a good deal more about, especially as we debate the future of libraries in a world of changing technology and economic organization. To understand the processes and structures whereby people have created and communicated knowledge, historians need to go beyond traditional institutional boundaries and conventional thinking about institutions and ask questions that can reveal the connections between the so-called storehouses and workshops of knowledge and knowledge itself, the "actual structure of the historical interdependence of libraries and scholarship," as the British librarian Ian Willison puts it.[15] They need to explore further the role of information systems in acquiring and producing knowledge, and all within intellectual, institutional, and social contexts. My aim in this paper is to raise several of these questions, suggest hypotheses for further exploration, and offer illustrations, with particular reference to research libraries during the era of the rise of the American university, and with consideration of urban public libraries as scholarly resources.

ACADEMIC LIBRARIES IN THE AGE OF THE COLLEGE

In the development of collections in support of scholarship and science in the United States, university libraries became really significant only in the twentieth century. Until the late nineteenth century, academic collections, though growing, were on the whole modest and inadequate for extensive research projects; what scholarly resources there were in the United States existed, except for Harvard and Yale, mostly elsewhere, in public and society libraries of various sorts and in private collections, and even these were limited. Before the Civil War there were decent collections of standard literature, but no great accumulations such as scholars might use in western Europe, with its heritage of royal, princely, and ecclesiastical collections as sources for university and national libraries. American intellectuals had to import from Europe most scholarly books and journals, or go there to see them. The Federalist politician Fisher Ames early in the nineteenth century provided us with the often quoted yet still pithy view of American scholarly resources: to write the history of "any foreign nation where could an American author collect his materials and authorities? Few persons reflect, that all our universities would not suffice to supply them for such a work as Gibbon's."[16] Scientists were equally despairing about scientific books, which were scarce almost everywhere and nowhere sufficient. In 1846 James Dana, geologist for the United States South Seas Exploring Expedition, found it "perfectly absurd" to think of working on his specimens in Washington, "a city where there are no books"; and Louis Agassiz wrote in 1855 that no one "has felt more keenly the want of an extensive scientific library than I have since I have been in the United States."[17] Legal, historical, and learned societies had some specialized holdings, and the larger general subscription or society libraries, like the Boston Athenaeum (founded in 1807), had materials for study, but altogether resources for research and higher learning were in short supply.

The situation began to improve after mid-century, thanks in part to the efforts of Americans who had been impressed by the extensive collections organized in Europe, especially in Germany, to support the new modern scholarship. George Ticknor and his fellow students abroad, Edward Everett and Joseph Green Cogswell, tried to bring Harvard College into the nineteenth century, intellectually speaking, and to introduce new pedagogy into education for elite boys—all without much result at the time. But they did succeed in creating before the Civil War two new types of American libraries, both opened in 1854 and both important as scholarly collections.

Cogswell, schoolmaster and onetime Harvard librarian, is said to have persuaded the close-fisted old nabob John Jacob Astor to bequeath part of his great fortune to establish in 1848 the Astor Library in New York

City, which had no substantial general library. As its first director, Cogswell developed this first privately endowed free reference library in the United States, predecessor of the New York Public Library, into a comprehensive, cosmopolitan collection that from the beginning stood among the best in the country. Though open to the public, it was for in-house research and study only, a policy arising in part out of Cogswell's snobbishness and interest only in what he deemed serious literature. But the policy also made sense in an era of bibliothecal scarcity and it did, at least in principle, democratize access to scholarly libraries.

Up in Boston, Cogswell's friends Ticknor, a scholar and bibliophile, and Everett, a classicist and statesman, were instrumental in founding, soon after the Astor, another new library model: the Boston Public Library, the first tax-supported municipal library in the United States. Designed to be used for serious study as well as for popular education, the Boston Public Library developed a distinguished research collection, which, unlike the elite, private Boston Athenaeum, was open freely to the public.[18] Out of somewhat different cultural and political influences—earlier French and British ideas and attitudes, and interest in nation building and state enterprise—came the budding national library, the Library of Congress. Based on the private collection of our man of the Enlightenment, Thomas Jefferson, the Library of Congress would gradually, through the efforts of Ainsworth Rand Spofford, Librarian from 1864 to 1897, become a general research collection.[19]

Academic libraries, excepting Harvard and Yale and a few others, were as undistinguished and arid as the colleges themselves, although historians' views of the early colleges have become more charitable, and some of the colleges had less narrow library collections than had been thought.[20] The state universities were either still quite undeveloped or yet to be born as land grant colleges under the Morrill Act of 1862. And even at the Yales and Harvards, which were slowly moving away from classicism, students had to acquire on their own literature on burning issues of the day. The lively debating and literary societies within which college students fashioned the alternative, extracurricular culture that was so important to their education developed substantial libraries that prefigured and later served as the basis for modern undergraduate college collections. More significantly, the society libraries influenced students' thinking. Historian James McLachlan, in a study that includes an analysis of students' reading in an early nineteenth-century Princeton society, concludes that the societies, by molding the ideals and ideas of "thousand of youths," helped powerfully to create the "neohumanistic man of letters of 19th century America" who, "equipped with a profound faith in the power of oratory, of the pen, and of the printed word," conceived of himself "as a culture-shaping hero, bent on the reformation of society."[21] The first general index to periodicals, published in 1848, was devised at a Yale literary society, Brothers in Unity, by a student librarian, William F. Poole, in order to give the members access to the contents of current periodicals. The success of this work led Poole into libraries instead of the law, and he rose to leadership of the new profession of librarianship in the United States.[22]

In 1876, the extensive library development that followed economic and population growth in the country was celebrated in the United States Bureau of Education's classic centennial compendium on American libraries of every kind, *Public Libraries in the United States of America*, which showed substantial growth in the number and types of libraries and in scholarly resources.[23] As for academic libraries, Edward G. Holley, in a masterly retrospective assessment written a hundred years after the 1876 report, concludes that they were in 1876 "small, but expanding": contrary to traditional notions, many academic libraries, in response to changes in higher education, were striving toward significance in the educational process, toward making libraries "a vital part of college experience."[24]

Compared, however, to the best European libraries—national libraries like the British Museum and the Bibliothèque Nationale, the leading German university collections, and the Bodleian at Oxford—American collections still had a long way to go as tools for scholarship. This inadequacy was particularly acute in the sciences, especially in academe, where science had not been an important area of study or research; even standard manuals, proceedings, journals, and handbooks were not to be found in the United States.[25] It was to remedy this situation in the field of medicine that John Shaw Billings, the distinguished physician, librarian, and bibliographer, undertook after the Civil War to create the comprehensive United States Army Surgeon-General's Library (now the National Library of Medicine) and produce its great *Index-Catalogue* and the *Index Medicus*.[26]

Billings's program for identifying and obtaining medical works, which William Welch of John Hopkins in 1913 called "probably the most original and distinctive contribution of America to the medicine of the world,"[27] exemplifies a point made by John Higham about the growth of scholarship and of access to knowledge at the turn of the century. Higham contends that in the large, sprawling, diverse, and relatively democratic United States, this expansion, in the absence of an intellectual or scientific center or primary authority, led to the development of formal bibliographic devices—indexes, catalogs, and directories—to control the outpouring of literature and to make knowledge of it widely available.[28]

It is interesting that this bibliographic control was effected on the whole in a dichotomous way in United States institutions. In contrast to Billings's total system, twentieth-century libraries retained the functions of acquiring materials, recording their holdings in catalogs, and arranging them systematically on shelves; private companies and learned societies, on the other hand, took on the task of producing bibliographies, indexes, and abstracts.[29] The proliferation of the latter reference works for scholars reflected the centrifugal specialization that Higham sees as the hallmark of the intellectual transformation at the turn of the century. Through their wide-ranging acquisitions and the new card catalogs, which became centralized, codified records of holdings that were often decentralized on a sprawling campus, the libraries served in a sense as unifying, centripetal forces. This function is enhanced in our time on an extraordinary national and international basis by computer and telecommunications technology. James Beniger, in a recent book equating modernism with the creation and imposition of devices and systems to control economic processes, calls the late nineteenth-century librarians "the first information scientists" in devising systems to control their collections and files.[30]

LIBRARIES AND THE TRANSFORMATION OF HIGHER EDUCATION

As American universities began to move to center stage as institutions vital to modern society, rather than as enclaves of gentlemanly learning and Christian character building or as provincial "cow colleges," their libraries began a steep move upward in holdings. True, the climb was fitful and rocky, and until after World War II, only a few northeastern, midwestern, and Californian centers of research and education approached the heights. The spectacular nationwide library growth during the "academic revolution"[31] of the post–World War II years lay ahead, and before then American libraries had notable lacunae. Even so, given the fact that so many universities with large ambitions were starting virtually from the bottom, the increase in resources of all sorts during the first half of the twentieth century was impressive, as were the monumental (if not always functional) library buildings erected on campuses as well as in municipalities.[32]

The rise of university libraries corresponded with the transformation and growth of scholarship and science and of their institutional bases, as well as the expansion in publishing. Edward Shils writes in discussing the ascendancy of the university:

Those institutions whose members regarded study and teaching as their major obligation came to be recognized as the primary instruments for the cultivation of learning in America. In the decades following the end of the Civil War, the productive scholars and scientists of the United States increasingly became members of academic institutions. Instead of relying on their own financial resources and carrying out their work at home or in the private libraries of learned societies, the new scholars and scientists gained their livelihood primarily through employment by a college or university, using the books, journals, laboratories, and equipment provided by these institutions.[33]

The change was also quantitative: there were many more students, undergraduate and graduate both, and more professors, a trend that accelerated in the 1920s.

If the university presidents and boards of trustees who presided over these developments seem to have been at the beginning less committed to research (and libraries) than to building and managing academic empires of service to the existing social system, leading faculty members were imbued with the idea of the university as intellectual wellspring. They esteemed the free, secular, disinterested pursuit of knowledge that many of them had seen in the best German universities. The rise of modern science and of positivist approaches generally, together with the German historicists' focus on documentary sources and the American Progressive belief in knowledge as essential to solving social and political problems, as well as the accompanying growth of graduate education, all pointed to the need for extensive collections of library materials along with laboratories and seminar rooms. The new commitment to the spirit of inquiry, writes historian Frederick Rudolph, "meant that the universities expressed their purposes no longer in the chapel," nor in the president's seminar on moral and intellectual philosophy. That seminar "was now a half-dozen subjects spread throughout the curriculum, and beginning to overshadow the chapel itself were the science laboratories and the libraries, as necessary to the new dispensation as the chapel had been to the old."[34]

All this would be expensive, which meant that the smaller institutions would have trouble providing the new resources. Even the best and richest institutions would have perpetually to search for money, in a society where the competition for funds for all sorts of public enterprises became unremitting and the importance of academic research had yet to be firmly established. The desperate need at Harvard for more library space apparently led President Charles W. Eliot to contemplate throwing out library books (a dilemma luckily resolved with the Widener gift of a library building in 1912).[35] Still, Eliot did envision universities as having three main functions: "In the first place they teach; secondly, they accumulate great stores of acquired and systematized knowledge in the form of books and collections; thirdly, they investigate."[36]

Roger Geiger, in his recent book on the growth of American research universities from 1900 to 1940 (whose comparative approach could well be a model for a study of research libraries), observes that the system of universities taking shape at the turn of the century encompassed interrelated, complex trends, each of which "developed according to its own internal logic and momentum" and which, "being substantially interrelated, . . . powerfully reinforced one another once they were in place."[37] Their libraries, one suspects, developed somewhat similarly, with their own internal dynamics and with reinforcement from other elements in the university varying from one place to another. The extent to which Eliot's three functions of the university—teaching, library development, and investigation—intersected is a question that deserves further investigation, and on a comparative basis. In a number of institutions the faculty for a long time kept a great measure of control over the library through power over book selection; but that might not ensure that library development would be organically and systematically integrated with scholarly endeavors (which themselves evolved unevenly). The real work of collection building and the direct intellectual impetus for it rested, I would hypothesize, with a relatively few, if deeply interested, faculty members and, eventually, strong dedicated librarians, though of course levels of commitment to the library would differ from place to place and time to time.[38] Library resources and services may have come to function as nodes in scholarly communication, but as universities became large-scale, complex operations the library stood apart institutionally on the campus. Though not autonomous, it came to constitute a discrete social system within the social system of the university.

The growth of libraries and their evolution into extensive systems needing professionally trained librarians to run them meant also that librarians would in time create their own, unique culture, and that they would strongly identify with professional library specialties and the larger professional community of academic librarianship. This phenomenon was a feature of the professionalization taking place in all of scholarship and science—the creation, in Bender's words, of a "community without locality" that impelled the increasingly research-oriented faculty to turn their loyalties toward subject specialties and professional groups.[39] In librarianship, the process may well have been intensified by problems of status and authority that librarians suffered in the university environment. Librarians saw their profession as playing a key role in the educational and research process, but were not able sufficiently to articulate a unique, socially significant mission and convince others of its worth and power. They yearned for recognition as academic colleagues of the faculty, but rarely achieved it. In our time, although the concept of faculty status for librarians has been endorsed by the library profession and by the American Association of University Professors, and although librarians have achieved such status in a number of universities, it is questionable whether real equality exists, and the issue of faculty status remains controversial among research librarians.[40]

The literature of the history of libraries and librarianship has begun to deal with these issues, which pertain to the essence of libraries and librarianship and demand thoughtful investigation and analysis. For example, in a revisionist study of the origins of American academic librarianship to 1920, Lee Shiflett explores the frustrations, lack of power, and low status of academic librarians.[41] During the early years, before the late nineteenth century, the library, while having a certain symbolic value on the campus, did not seem to be very significant. At that time the college curriculum was classical or theological or both; teaching and learning involved lectures and prescribed texts and recitations; and faculty members were not expected to engage in research. Librarians stood at the bottom of the academic status ladder.[42] This situation did not greatly improve when colleges began to change and library collections became relevant to the mission of the new universities. The directorship of libraries would then more likely as not go to a faculty member rather than a member of the new profession of librarianship. In 1927, a study done for the Association of American Universities of academic library problems concluded that professional librarians below the rank of head or assistant librarian were often regarded as little more than clerks.[43] The association of librarianship with women and femininity that became widespread at the turn of the century, along with the cruel stereotypes, might have had some part here. This matter is not simple, for, in contrast to public librarians but consonant with the predominantly male world of academe, many academic librarians were male, which was certainly the case in the highest, most prestigious positions (as in large public libraries as well). Women did run a number of midwestern academic libraries, but by the mid-1930s nearly all research university library directors were male, as were most deputy and assistant directors; these figures were disproportionate to the male-female ratio in the library profession as a whole. This state of affairs began to change only during the 1970s and 1980s under the influence of the women's movement and affirmative action programs.[44]

At best the professional librarians who began to staff academic libraries in the early twentieth century were seen as technicians and managers, not, as many would have liked, peers of the faculty, as scholars and intellectuals who would shape collections, guide students' reading, and deal with the academic administration, faculty departments, and prospective donors. Shiflett concludes, as of the 1920s, that there was a conflict between academic librarians' professional ideology and the research-oriented new universities. The librarians' view of themselves derived from the predominant public library ideology in the American Library Association (ALA), founded in 1876 as one of the first American professional associations. The ALA ideology proclaimed libraries as educational, service agencies and librarians as having control over collections. In the universities, education was a matter for the faculty, whose status and success would be increasingly measured by their research productivity, an activity to which libraries would contribute, but with faculty members as book selectors and librarians as organizers, often under the direction of a chief afted from the faculty.⁴⁵ Even when professionally trained ook over the field as library directors in the mid-twentieth century, argument over whether they should be scholars or librarians , as it does to this day. This theme runs through a recently published collection of biographical essays on fifteen American academic library leaders active between 1925 and 1975. The essays also indicate the low level of university library management that existed when these men and women, most of them professionally trained in library schools and active in the new associations founded exclusively to deal with academic library concerns, came on the scene (mainly in the 1930s and 1940s) to modernize and professionalize academic libraries.⁴⁶

As for the university library collections built by various persons and groups, they reflected varying concepts of the nature of research libraries, as library historians point out. In the nineteenth century several approaches emerged. One was the idea of a "universal research library" as "a comprehensive collection of the most important writings of all times and all nations in all branches of learning," the nineteenth-century German university model. Another view conceived a universal research library in broader terms, as aiming to keep pace with advancing knowledge and to serve as a source for both present and future research by preserving the myriad documentation of humankind. The latter was the national library model, based in part on the Bibliothèque Nationale and developed by the great director of the British Museum in the Victorian Age, Antonio Panizzi, and encompassing the idea of free public access. Both concepts derived from Enlightenment ideas of the value of rational knowledge to society.⁴⁷ And both differ from the notion of smaller bodies of materials carefully chosen as vehicles of education either for undergraduate students or the general public. In American academe, these various ideas about libraries can be seen as mirroring the several and sometimes conflicting missions of the modern university, as it evolved from an institution devoted to inculcating moral and social values and transmitting traditional knowledge to an institution also concerned with preserving knowledge and fostering the discovery and creation of new knowledge.

The American university, unlike the European, came to take within its purview just about every intellectual endeavor and professional calling. Virtually everything could come under the guiding principle termed by Geiger "cognitive rationality," the principle of "knowing through the exercise of reason," in the service of pure intellect or in direct usefulness to society.⁴⁸ The result was a multipurpose institution, with struggles, still with us, over the merits of teaching versus research; general education versus professional education; general culture versus specialization; selectivity versus comprehensiveness; and undergraduate versus graduate education. The university library, in principle the servant of its parent institution, in time attempted to do everything. Besides collecting research publications in general, libraries came to provide undergraduate collections of standard and "best" works;

general collections for graduate study; reserve book rooms for classroom assignments; specialized departmental and professional school libraries; collections of manuscripts and other rare materials; and, in the 1930s, "browsing rooms," clublike settings with newspapers, magazines, and current books. They offered instruction in library use to undergraduates, and in research resources to graduate students; some university libraries gave individualized help with research and study, with the doyenne of American reference librarians, Isadore Mudge, leading the way at Columbia.[49]

COLLECTION DEVELOPMENT IN ACADEMIC LIBRARIES

Libraries would have to balance all these functions and at the same time focus on the resources for which they, and their parent universities, would gain prestige and praise—the research collections. They had to do it alone, more or less, and, in many places, with never enough money. There were important cooperative ventures among research libraries before the mid-twentieth century: interlibrary loan, publication of the *Union List of Serials* in 1927, the National Union Catalog at the Library of Congress, and regional union catalogs. During the late 1920s and in the national planning environment of the 1930s, proposals were made for interlibrary cooperation to share resources and improve national coverage, but without practical results.[50] It took the World War II experience in intelligence gathering and the problems of obtaining books and journals from Europe to propel research libraries into the first major programs to build collections jointly.[51] These were the Cooperative Acquisitions Project for Wartime Publications, which brought nearly two million pieces from Europe to American research libraries, and the Farmington Plan, devised to insure that monographic publications of research value from all over the world would be in at least one American library; the war had shown great gaps in holdings of foreign materials. In 1949, the Midwest Inter-Library Center in Chicago (now the Center for Research Libraries), a library's library, was founded for cooperative storage and acquisition of little-used materials. And, of course, university librarians did join together in organizations to discuss common problems. Nevertheless, until quite recently, when economic pressures and technological advances combined to change the outlook of research librarians, their collections, like their parent institutions, developed on the whole autonomously, unevenly, and not always systematically.

Several library historians have been especially interested in collection development for academe. Charles Osburn, in a thoughtful book on academic research and library resources after World War II, maintains that university libraries traditionally acquired scientific and social scientific materials less actively than humanistic resources, and continued to do so even as the balance in publishing and research support shifted toward the sciences and social sciences.[52] A study of Yale's library from 1855 to 1931 by Thomas O'Connor supports this thesis in relation to curriculum and to postgraduate and faculty research. O'Connor shows that in general there was not much direct intersection between library programs and university programs; a few professors were deeply interested in the library, but in an institution heavily dependent on gifts, the major influence on collections came from donors' interests.[53] On the other hand, Wayne Yenawine's earlier study of the influence of scholars on the development of research collections from 1900 to 1930 at the University of Illinois, a state university striving for distinction, demonstrates close connections between these collections and the growth of scholarship at the university, along with significant faculty involvement in a successful program of collection building. There was at Illinois strong professional library leadership; sustained, liberal support from a university administration determined to create a research institution; and faculty interest, especially among the most productive scholars, in systematic acquisitions.[54]

In their broad survey of collection development in American universities from 1876 to 1976, Hendrik Edelman and G. Marvin Tatum, Jr. discuss the surge in collecting at the turn of the century. They comment in regard to new journals and scientific proceedings that "the importance of systematically acquiring currently published material was only slowly recognized" and that even major American libraries' share of the accumulated world book production was "still rather modest." J. Periam Danton concludes from a comparative statistical analysis of selected major university libraries' book budgets in 1860, 1910, and 1960 that in relation to estimates of the total world book production and numbers of students and faculty members, expenditures for books were no greater in 1960 than earlier and possibly less than in 1860.[55]

Clearly additional research and comparative study need to be done. At this point it would seem that the great institutional ingathering of materials that began at the turn of the century represented something of a mix of the German and Panizzian models. Acquisitions occurred not always and not everywhere with the systematic, conscious planning of either of the originals, and it had uneven results. This was no doubt partly due to the need for librarians and concerned faculty members to search continually for money and gifts of collections, in some universities in competition with other campus interests, at a time when university administrators were struggling to build financial support for various components of their complex, growing institutions. In libraries and their parent universities, the new patterns set at the turn of the century can be seen as marking only the inauguration of modernization (itself the culmination of earlier trends). The actual transformation into strong research institutions would go on for several decades, with the top research universities (some sixteen) entering a "golden age" in 1930 and then, with others, reaching spectacular climax during the post–World War II decades.[56]

As for university libraries, although several did quite well and the effort to catch up with Europe was prodigal, if they had a golden age it probably came later, after the war. It appears that not until well into the twentieth century did reliance upon gifts in a number of institutions, including some of the leading ones, especially those under private auspices, give way to substantial regular general appropriations.[57] Various surveys during the late 1920s and 1930s indicated that a number of academic institutions offering graduate study had far to go in providing adequate library resources and in receiving consistent library budgets. Louis Round Wilson's classic survey *The Geography of Reading*, published in 1935, documented the uneven geographic distribution of research resources in the United States.[58]

In 1938, the Science Committee of the National Resources Committee, surveying research efforts in American academe, reported that eleven universities were granting more than half of all the American earned doctorates, thirty-two institutions the next forty percent, and forty-three, the last ten percent. The libraries of "eight of the great universities" were "adequate in all fields" to support research; ten more were approaching such a point, and ten others were making decent progress. The committee attributed the sorry library situation in the remainder of the institutions to the "clearly evident" fact that "the majority of college and university presidents and boards of trustees have no adequate conception of what a library should be in books, periodicals, and service in a modern educational institution."[59] The common (though not universal) practice of allocating money for book purchases to academic departments and responsibility for selection to faculty members, who would be erratically interested in the process, could mean, furthermore, that collecting might be unbalanced and incomplete. This situation was exacerbated by what has been called the "almost rapacious" acquisition by both gift or purchase of whole libraries of various sorts and sizes as they became available.[60]

Under the best of circumstances, completeness, even if accepted as a goal, was not and could not be achieved, and not only because of the practical impossibility of acquiring everything on every subject. In practice the concept reflected notions, or paradigms, of what constituted research materials, appropriate subjects, and worthwhile scholarship. There was a tendency to collect most heavily the literature of Western and ancient classical cultures, along with the documentation of governments and ruling elites of these cultures. The ways in which these materials were made available—in subject headings in card catalogs and classification of books on shelves, as well as through published bibliographies—also reflected contemporary, and in time, frozen world views. Dewey's classification, for example, ingenious and practical as it was, expressed in its content and arrangement a mid-nineteenth-century, white, Protestant, Anglo-Saxon, male view of knowledge that in its basic structure harked back to Francis Bacon's faculty psychology.[61]

Scholars are today being drawn into decision making about preservation of library materials disintegrating on the shelves.[62] But they are already dealing with a fait accompli. They are determining whether to save or sacrifice material whose presence represents previous generations' notions of acceptability, and they themselves may well impose their own biases if they are not careful. One generation's trash is another's treasure. Witness the reprint and microprint projects and the new bibliographies that sprang up in the 1970s to support the contemporary interest in ethnicity, race relations, women, children, social deviance, and other subjects and groups, whose literature and documentation had not been systematically collected in most libraries either out of plain prejudice or because they were not in anyone's intellectual ken, not to speak of the absence of such topics from the curriculum.

It is probably true that libraries tend to reflect rather than create intellectual trends. It would be interesting nonetheless to know how, and if, availability of resources and the ways they were organized actually affected the interests and outputs of scholars—in other words, to study seriously the intellectual origins and impact of library collections and operations, through time, and comparatively, across disciplines and institutions. And conversely, it would also be interesting to learn to what extent information about or impressions of the use of materials influenced the acquisition and disposition of collections. One might say that by definition research libraries are little-used collections;[63] recent studies of library use and of scholarly and scientific literature indicate that though there are differences among disciplines and subdisciplines, a comparatively few titles receive the most use quantitatively and that the invisible college is a potent, often preferred, scholarly communication device. Was that always true? What is use? Do we define it or assign it value in quantitative or qualitative terms?

A related issue that would bear investigating is that of intellectual freedom—the principle of unbiased collecting and unhampered use of collections. Intellectual freedom is a cornerstone of the professional ideology of librarianship today, and a subject of special concern to research librarians in the Reagan era as federal officials have tried to limit access to data and investigate individual use of library materials. Studies of the public library setting have revealed that librarians' current anticensorship, proprivacy stance, first formally expressed in the ALA's 1939 "Library Bill of Rights," evolved from the nineteenth-century belief in and practice of library censorship (conscious exclusion of materials on moral, religious, or political grounds), which took acute form during the World War I anti-German hysteria.[64] Where research libraries stood is not as well known; studies of academic freedom concentrate on the classroom and the professors.[65]

The questions remain, in any case, of the degree to which university libraries acquired materials mainly in support of local current research and study; or in relation to abstract concepts of the nature of a scholarly library; or haphazardly, subject to the vagaries of the budget, the book market, faculty interest, or donors' predilections. And what should be the university library's obligations to the immediate academic community and to the wider world of scholarship, both present and future? Some early librarians did ponder these questions, and the University of California at Berkeley had a formal, comprehensive acquisitions policy statement by 1931 (drawn up by a faculty committee),[66] but it would seem that librarians generally inclined more to the pragmatic than the theoretical. They began creating systematic bibliographic records early. Decades later, in the late 1930s, systematic analysis of library operations and collections began; in the 1940s the principle of written acquisitions policies or at least statements of collecting aims became a professional library tenet.

Only in the 1970s was the principle widely carried out in academic libraries, as part of a remarkable rationalization effort among research libraries coping with a new era of expansion of higher education and research and with extraordinary rises in the prices and number of publications. This so-called "quiet revolution," as it is termed by librarian Paul Mosher, involved librarians assuming primary responsibility for collection development, for which they would write detailed policies, with faculty consultation.[67] For the actual selection of materials it became the fashion by the 1970s to appoint specialist librarian-bibliographers. This practice was haltingly attempted in a few American universities in the 1950s, and was advocated in 1963 by J. Periam Danton in a perceptive comparison of America and German university libraries, where such specialists had long been common.[68]

PUBLIC LIBRARIES AND SUPPORT OF RESEARCH

That mode of systematic, clearly purposeful, in-house selection had been the rule at another sort of "universal" research library outside of academe, and with outstanding results. The effectiveness of such collecting was graphically shown in 1936 in a classic study by Douglas Waples and Harold Lasswell of foreign social science holdings of leading American research libraries. The New York Public Library, without faculty members to select books, without legal deposit (such as the Library of Congress, the British Museum, and several British universities had), and with less money for acquisitions than the university libraries, led in all categories;

other studies showed similar findings.[69] The New York Public Library referred to here is its research wing, today called The Research Libraries, as distinguished from the separately financed local branch circulating library system (The Branch Libraries). Privately run and supported by endowments, gifts, and government aid of various kinds, the New York Public Library is one of the great libraries of the world, traditionally second in the United States to the Library of Congress (whose role in scholarship is the subject of John Cole's chapter in this volume and thus not considered here).

The New York Public Library is not a typical public library: it is unique in the scope and magnitude of its research collections, and indeed The Research Libraries are often classified among private independent libraries (whose considerable contributions to scholarship deserve serious study).[70] The New York Public Library is perhaps sui generis. Still, the complex relationships that it has always had with government—including shared ownership of assets with New York City and a mix of private and public financial support—along with the comprehensiveness and variety of the collections and their accessibility, justify the designation of public library (which was the founders' view).[71] Among public libraries it has not been alone in having research holdings, but New York's are the largest. The Boston Public Library, founded in part as Boston's answer to the New York Public Library's ancestor, the Astor Library, was and is still a leading research institution. Both libraries were distinctively American in being freely and immediately open to the public. Other public libraries established subsequently also developed substantial general and special collections for research use: for example, Cleveland, Philadelphia, Detroit, Buffalo, and St. Louis.

In fact such collecting was originally considered a public library responsibility, at a time when urban communities served as the prime sites for cultural and intellectual life. Reports of holdings that were published in the 1876 Bureau of Education report bear out this thesis, and several articles therein observed that the acquisition of materials for researchers and to document contemporary life was the function of public rather than academic libraries. The editors of the report, writing on "College Libraries," said that the latter "should be regarded as instruments to be kept in use, rather than as precious treasures to be stored up"; it was the public libraries in large towns "in which the attempt is made to bring together, and hand down to those who come after us, all the publications of our day and of past times."[72] In the article "Free Libraries," J. P. Quincy (presumably Josiah Quincy, the historian and member of the Quincy family prominent in Boston affairs, including the public library) although proclaiming that public libraries in small communities should be highly selective and even exercise "a reasonable censorship upon books," acknowledged that the libraries of "wealthy cities" could be justified in preserving "single copies of everything that comes to hand," including "silly, and even immoral, publications," which might offer illustrations to historians and give them "valuable aid in reproducing the life of the past."[73] Librarian of Congress Spofford and Justin Winsor, head of the Boston Public Library (and later of Harvard's library), urged that public libraries collect local history and genealogy materials, including newspapers, periodicals, pamphlets, broadsides, reports of organizations and governments, and other ephemera. These were, Winsor said, the "best reflex of the times."[74]

In the Midwest, cities anxious to have the appurtenances of culture sponsored public libraries as centers of both learning and popular reading. In Chicago, hub of the western book trade, the devastating fire of 1871 served as catalyst in founding the Chicago Public Library, for the purpose, among others and admittedly not a chief one, of encouraging scholarly pursuits. William F. Poole, director of the new library from 1874 to 1884, and initially interested in meeting needs for scholarship, complained to Justin Winsor in 1875 about the lack of research collections in Chicago, the "one drawback I feel of my residence in the West." Only by "providing the necessary appliances which literary men must have," could the city achieve the goal of "cultivating a literature, and a popular literary taste in the West," Poole wrote in his first annual report. Chicago meant to have a great, an "immense" library.[75] These ambitions were not fulfilled: the Chicago Public Library did get a fine building, opened in 1897, but it did not become a midwestern research library center, though it had some scholarly resources. In 1897 an informal agreement went into effect—with mixed results as time went on—between the Chicago Public Library and two new privately endowed reference libraries, the Newberry (largely for humanities) and the John Crerar (for science and technology). Aiming to provide a total library program for the city, and with only the new University of Chicago as a potential academic research library resource, the three libraries divided up collecting responsibility, with the Newberry and Crerar taking on research resources and the Public Library taking, on the whole, the popular side.[76]

Another leading midwestern public library, The Minneapolis Public Library, established in 1885, was conceived as a scholarly as well as popular institution by its first librarian, Herbert Putnam (subsequently head of the Boston Public Library and then Librarian of Congress) and by his successor James K. Hosmer—both, like Poole, transplanted easterners. Predicting that a "literary class, a scholarly class; a class demanding products of continental scholarship at first hand" would emerge in the city, Putnam wanted to meet this demand and "uplift the Minneapolis library to the scholarly ranks of the great libraries of the East." That was not to be: Hosmer's dynamic successor, Gratia Countryman, focussed the library on popular services and educational uplift:

whether the growth in the city of the University of Minnesota was a factor here is not clear.[77] In Detroit, the public library, opened in 1865 and emphasizing popular education, eventually developed the strong reference, periodical, and special collections that made it, in its historian's words, the "significant—and only—major reference-research center in a vast metropolitan area."[78]

The exemplar in the United States of the German university idea, Johns Hopkins, which opened in 1876, was not at first intended to have a substantial general library. Rather it would rely upon small departmental libraries and other Baltimore collections—especially the Peabody Institute and the Maryland Historical Society, and then the new Enoch Pratt Free Library. This policy, which one historian sees as primarily "an adroit, cost-effective decision" by President Daniel Coit Gilman (a former Yale librarian) in face of the financial demands of creating a new university, was strongly supported by the influential history professor Herbert Baxter Adams, who had used seminar libraries in Germany. Evidently, though, Johns Hopkins could not get by entirely on this basis: at the end of the century the university had the tenth largest academic library in the country, although students and faculty continued to use other local libraries.[79]

By then the center of gravity of scholarly and scientific investigation was clearly moving to academe. But this was just the time that the New York Public Library was formed by the consolidation in 1895 of the Astor Library with the Lenox Library (an endowed reference collection of rarities and Americana) and the Tilden Trust (an endowment left by Samuel J. Tilden for a public library in New York City). The merger occurred in face of campaigns by powerful people in the city's two major academic institutions, Columbia and New York Universities (both named universities in 1896), to get the Tilden Trust's money for their own libraries, which needed buildings and books.[80] That they failed is telling not only of the skill, determination, and sophistication of the men who engineered the founding of the New York Public Library, but also of the nature of New York. As the nation's cultural mecca and most populous city, it would retain a rich and complex interplay of cultural and educational institutions and associations, well beyond academe.

In the 1890s, the Astor Library having fallen upon hard times, New York lacked, as contemporary commentators saw it, a great library commensurate with its status as first city of the nation. Columbia and New York University were just beginning to be transformed into universities, and unaffiliated, nonacademic intellectuals and information seekers abounded. City leaders, wanting to celebrate the metropolis's power, wealth, and culture, and supported by popular sentiment for the library as an educational agency, got the municipality to construct for the New York Public Library a splendid building that could compare with the much admired new Boston Public Library. Led by the first Director, John Shaw Billings, who had connections with important scientific and scholarly enterprises here and abroad, and who kept up with intellectual trends, the New York Public Library moved from Cogswell's German university model to the more inclusive Panizzi model. (Indeed in choosing a director the trustees said they were searching for a latter-day Panizzi.) The New York Public Library surpassed Panizzi's liberalism in its democratic, expansive policies toward collections and use: it became a vast repository open to everyone immediately and without question, every day and every evening of the year, with materials delivered to users in minutes (policies that would become, it must be said, sources of problems as well as strengths).[81]

Under Billings, and then for some forty years under Harry Miller Lydenberg (first head of the research library and then director of the entire institution from 1934 to 1941), the New York Public Library went far beyond collecting conventionally significant writings, to systematic acquisition of an enormous variety of materials. These included books, journals, pamphlets, newspapers, manuscripts, prints, pictures, music, domestic and foreign government documents, memorabilia, the documents of a wide range of organizations and associations, and audio-visual materials. Within the fields chosen to cover, as expressed in a general statement of 1901 and in subsequent statements, the library aimed at comprehensiveness, with certain areas—medicine, law, pedagogy, and biological sciences—left to other strong libraries in the city.[82]

Without a faculty's interests to consider and not having to deal with faculty members' rival role in selecting books, Lydenberg and his staff (several of whom went on to become distinguished university librarians) could develop a more or less balanced approach to collecting. They took into consideration the whole of knowledge, past and present (as they saw it), and recognized that the world of knowledge transcended academe. The library competed with other agencies for private gifts and municipal and state funds, but it had no internal contenders for money—no football stadiums, faculty salaries, or laboratory equipment to worry about—and no curriculum or research grants to accommodate. It also had no potentially protective institutional superstructure. There was of course a politics of the library, but it was different from that of the university. The New York Public Library was a self-contained institution run by professional librarians. The chief librarian had direct access to the trustees, a group of rich, powerful, elderly white men who respected the professionalism of the librarians and confined themselves to policy making and money management, and who before World War II would make up deficits out of their pockets or through contacts with other rich men.

Until that time, despite financial ups and downs, the librarians managed to keep up acquisitions. They were in their collecting very much aware of current affairs and current intellectual and social trends, including controversial issues, and they had a strong concern for posterity. The library was seen as a great social archive as well as a species of scholarly academy. There was also a commitment to support scientific and technological investigation. Science, and particularly basic science, increasingly came under the aegis of the university, but there was still a good deal of scientific and technical research conducted in the private sector, and some individuals continued to pursue their own scientific interests with the help of public libraries. The New York Public Library's favorite example of the latter is its role in supplying Chester Carlson with information leading to his invention of xerography.

Subjects and materials that many universities might not have collected, or at least not collected significantly, were covered at the Public Library: for example, non-Western languages and cultures; the performing arts; graphic art; business information; and radical movements.[83] The trustees, directors, and librarians, whatever their own political or moral views—which certainly among the trustees and top library management inclined toward the conservative—took on the whole a modern, liberal, indeed libertarian stance toward research collections. All understood that in a great library of record (as opposed to the local branch circulating libraries where there were highly selective collections) anything and everything could be acquired, and from any place and any source. There was also concern to preserve confidentiality of readers, and few if any restraints were placed on what could be read except in the interest of preserving rare or fragile materials. The only consistently sensitive subjects in relation to the research library seem to have been erotica and sex hygiene, which were not listed in the public catalog and readily available until the mid-twentieth century. And in 1917, during World War I, there was a library policy that authorized reporting cases of readers requesting materials suspected of being "used in the interest of the enemies of the United States" to Federal authorities; in the 1940s, readers suspected of using library material in aid of espionage or subversive activities were so reported.[84]

The New York Public Library's catholicity in collecting flourished in the most cosmopolitan and sophisticated community in the country. If there were no faculty members or university administrators to consider, there were artists, designers, musicians, dancers, theater people, publishers, advertising researchers, writers, businessmen, inventors, political activists, and other groups vital to the city's strong pulse, people whose interests and needs for information the library felt bound to respect.

A particularly interesting facet of this responsiveness was the development of ethnic research collections, at a time when most universities were fitfully, if at all, acquiring such materials. In answer to requests from the large, intellectually active Russian and Jewish communities in New York, and with significant financial help from them, the Slavonic and Jewish Divisions were organized at the turn of the century. The first became one of the most important Slavic collections in the country, strengthened by a trip in 1923-24 to Eastern Europe and to postrevolutionary Russia by Lydenberg and the chief of the Slavonic Division, the scholar Avrahm Yarmolinsky. Academic institutions like Harvard and Stanford, as well as the Library of Congress, were also beginning to build up Slavic holdings, so that the New York Public Library was not alone in the field.[85] By contrast, the Jewish Division, as a special collection of materials documenting the life of the Jewish people, was probably unique at the time in the United States. It was established long before ethnic studies became fashionable in academe, and in spite of what can be construed as a certain amount of ethnic prejudice typical of their class and time among the predominantly Protestant trustees, who until at least the 1920s relied heavily upon gifts from the Jewish community to support the division.[86]

Another ethnic collection unusual for its time in a public library, or in any white-dominated institution (the first nonwhite New York Public Library trustees were elected in 1970) was the Schomburg Collection, the basis for the present Schomburg Center for Research in Black Culture. The collection was purchased in 1926 for the 135th Street Branch (later named for poet Countee Cullen) by the Carnegie Corporation at the urging of the National Urban League. Historian and bibliophile Arthur Schomburg's accumulation of rare materials on the peoples of Africa and the African diaspora figured in the Harlem Renaissance of the 1920s. In this flowering of black art, music, literature, politics, and culture, the entire library branch (under the leadership of liberal white librarian Ernestine Rose) served as gathering place and resource for black intellectuals. The history of the Schomburg Center is complex and problematic. It is intertwined with the history of Harlem and of Afro-Americans generally, as well as its place within the New York Public Library; throughout its vicissitudes, though, it remained for scholars a preeminent collection.[87]

Other specialties of the New York Public Library were the performing arts and the graphic arts, for which the city was the nation's capital. Music scores and musicology had been collected since Lenox Library days; later, systematic attention to music holdings made the collection a premier one in the United States, second only to the Library of Congress.[88] The other performing arts collections, all of which since 1965 have been components of the Lincoln Center for the Performing Arts, grew out of various gifts and the interest of the city's theater community, and then of efforts of curators to document the theater and dance. Performing arts programs on university campuses were mainly a post–World War II phenomenon and, except for music, probably would not be extensively represented in most retrospective academic library collections. The same could no doubt be said of the graphic arts. The New York Public Library had the first public print room in an American public library and the first in New York City (the Metropolitan Museum of Art did not open a print room until 1916); in developing this collection the library took the view, current among historians today, that etchings, woodcuts, and lithographs were social documents as well as esthetic objects.

The New York Public Library's use by scholars and intellectuals was phenomenal. The trustees and librarians loved to boast about surpassing the Library of Congress and the British Museum in numbers of readers, and survey after survey showed the dependence on the library by students and researchers of all kinds, as did testimonials and acknowledgments in countless books. For some researchers the library served virtually as their office. Years before the opening of the Frederick Lewis Allen Room in 1958 and the Wertheim Study in 1963 as workplaces for long-term users, efforts were made to provide for such persons. When the central building opened in 1911, certain researchers could use typewriters in special rooms; Willa Cather worked on her historical novels in a little office; and some researchers were accommodated in special study rooms. The Jewish Division was a virtual headquarters for the compilers of the monumental *Jewish Encyclopedia* and the *Universal Jewish Encyclopedia*; during World War I refuge was given to the great Hebraist, Eliezer ben Yehuda of Jerusalem.[89]

Although the New York Public Library has been very much a civic product and a local attraction, and although many of its special collections reflect the New York ambience, it has transcended localism to take on the universal quality of the great European national collections that inspired its founders. In the magnitude, quality, and significance of its holdings, and in the voluminous catalogs describing them, the New York Public Library has always served larger interests and clienteles. And as an institution and through the staff's activities, it has been involved in virtually all the major bibliographical and bibliothecal enterprises in the United States. It was a charter member (as was the Boston Public Library) of the Association of Research Libraries (formed in 1932) and of the influential consortium The Research Libraries Group (1974). Under Lydenberg's leadership, the New York Public Library pioneered in preserving newspapers and other materials and disseminated information about its resources through its *Bulletin* and an active publishing program.

Rooted in New York, and sharing the city's vibrancy and vicissitudes, it has also been a national, and international, library power. In that role the New York Public Library, as an independent organization, did not seem to suffer from some of the tensions that university libraries face as subordinate parts of parent institutions. Not only was the staff free to run the library and choose the books, and without anxieties about academic status, but in its autonomous embrace of eclecticism and universality, the New York Public Library was spared the problem of balancing in its collections local academic and global interests, or of weighing immediate academic demands against potential future demands. The issue of localism did come into play in other ways, probably most acutely in maintaining levels of financial support. The people of the city, and often its public officials, did not easily understand the library's dual functions of supporting both research and the use of popular materials in two virtually separate systems, or the need for massive funds for both, especially as the total enterprise was governed by a self-perpetuating board of trustees, albeit with municipal representatives. And it took some time for the library aggressively to promote itself as a national as well as local resource that merited wide public and private support.

Public libraries in some other cities, though not as heavily devoted to research resources as the New York Public Library and not nearly as big, continued to collect such materials even after academic institutions took responsibility to develop libraries in support of research and advanced study. In the early twentieth century, urban public libraries did come to concentrate on popular education and information services—witness the Chicago and Minneapolis examples, among others. But that was not all.[90] University library development was uneven, and in some cases there was a measure of cooperation in collecting between them and neighboring large public libraries (including Minneapolis). As higher education enrollments multiplied in the 1920s, the public library in some cities might in effect subsidize local colleges and universities by providing materials and help to students and faculty members. This became a critical problem in New York, but was evident elsewhere as well, especially as curricular changes reduced reliance on texts and as more and larger graduate programs were launched, often without proportionate academic library growth. Studies of public library use have always shown disproportionate numbers of students among clienteles.[91] There remained, furthermore, unaffiliated persons in search of extensive information and in pursuit of learning whom public libraries continued to serve. At a time when modern enterprises increasingly needed information but when corporate and other special libraries were still scarce, some urban libraries tried to fill the gap. Public libraries also responded to local interests in developing specialized reference collections, and they were hospitable to all sorts of gifts.

This is a subject requiring more research, but one can even now cite a few examples outside New York City: the Denver Public Library amassed a strong collection of Western Americana; the Cleveland Public Library had the John G. White Department of Orientalia, Folklore, and Chess; the Carnegie Library of Pittsburgh had a strong technology department, the first in an American public library; Detroit specialized in science and technology, automotive history, and genealogy; the Free Library of Philadelphia had an extensive store of orchestral scores and theater materials, as well as a noted rare book room; the Boston Public Library retained among its many research strengths a print collection; the Los Angeles Public Library developed a collection on film and theater; the Enoch Pratt Free Library in Baltimore, a favorite of H. L. Mencken, received his personal papers. The largest libraries were depositories for United States government documents, and many had patent collections; and the Progressive movement at the turn of century, involving as it did the appeal to reason and knowledge as a basis for responsible government, spawned municipal reference or legislative libraries in a number of public libraries before World War I. And whatever else was or was not collected for scholarly use, there were materials on local history, which continued to be seen as the province of the public library.[92]

The Great Depression, which hit public libraries hard, no doubt inhibited purchase of specialized materials, but the Works Progress Administration did enable libraries in some cities to engage in rather extensive cooperative scholarly bibliographic projects, particularly in aid of local history, and to join in creating regional union catalogs, which were called upon by academics and students.[93] In fact, the presence of research level materials became a serious problem for inner-city libraries later, during the 1970s, with the growth of the suburbs, downtown urban blight, and eventually, improvement in academic and other libraries.[94] Unlike people, books do not move away. The library community's response has been, in theory and to an extent in practice, to develop multitype regional library networks in recognition of the mix of institutional collections and the realities of modern metropolitan life.

Libraries and librarianship have a life of their own, diverse and complex, at the same time as they are creatures of the intellectual and social structures and environments in which they function and whose existence they document through their collections. It is these intricate and problematic relationships, through time and across time, in one place and in many places, that need to be probed carefully and thoughtfully. I have here looked briefly at a few of these relationships and raised questions about others, as cases in point, to suggest and illustrate how the historical roles of libraries and librarians in scholarly enterprises can be meaningfully addressed. Libraries can be seen variously as organizations, with their own bureaucracies, politics, and professional culture; as ideological and intellectual expressions and symbols; as architectural visions; as machines to organize and deliver information. Such approaches, beyond yielding more sophisticated understandings of libraries, offer new ways of viewing the broader world of scholarship and science and the institutions and professions involved with them. Someday someone will integrate all this, will fill in the "matrix for research." Meanwhile, our separate explorations, informed by awareness of this matrix, can enrich intellectual and institutional history and lend perspective and insight to contemplation of the future of libraries, our intellectual legacies from the past.

NOTES

1. "George Ticknor on the Inadequacy of American Libraries, 1816" (George Ticknor, letter to Stephen Higginson, Göttingen, May 20, 1816), in *American Higher Education: A Documentary History*, ed. Richard Hofstadter and Wilson Smith (Chicago: University of Chicago Press, 1961) 1: 256.

2. Logan Wilson, *American Academics: Then and Now* (New York: Oxford University Press, 1979) 215, 227-28.

3. *ALA Yearbook of Library and Information Services* (Chicago: American Library Association, 1988) 13: 62.

4. Thomas S. Kuhn, *The Structure of Scientific Revolutions*, 2d ed., International Encyclopedia of Unified Science, Foundations of the Unity of Science, vol. 2, no. 2 (Chicago: University of Chicago Press, 1970); I. Bernard Cohen, *Revolution in Science* (Cambridge, MA: Harvard University Press, Belknap Press, 1985) 28-31, 81-83; Derek J. de Solla Price, *Little Science, Big Science* (New York: Columbia University Press, 1963), chaps. 1-3; Derek J. de Solla Price, *Science Since Babylon* (New Haven: Yale University Press, 1961), chap. 5. Thomas L. Haskell, in *The Emergence of Professional Social Science: The American Social Science Association and the Nineteenth-Century Crisis of Authority* (Urbana: University of Illinois Press, 1977), applies, in a broad sense, Kuhn's theory of paradigmatic development. He discusses the nature of "community of the competent" in the professionalization process (65-68), and notes the role of means of communication and transportation in changing concepts of society; because his interest is elsewhere, he does not go into the role of intra-professional communication as a feature of professionalization.

5. Blanche H. Gelfant, "Panel Discussion," in *American Libraries as Centers of Scholarship; Proceedings of Convocation Held at Dartmouth College on June 30th, 1978*, ed. Edward Connery Lathem (Hanover, NH: Dartmouth College, 1978) 101.

6. Several works issued by non-library organizations in the 1960s and 1970s were concerned with libraries and scholarly communication. See American Council on Learned Societies (ACLS), Committee on Research Libraries, *On Research Libraries: Statement and Recommendations . . . Submitted to the National Advisory Commission on Libraries, 1967* (Cambridge, MA: MIT Press, 1969); *Research Universities and the National Interest: A Report from Fifteen University Presidents* (New York: Ford Foundation, 1978) 89-107; *Scholarly Communication: The Report of the National Enquiry* (Baltimore: Johns Hopkins University Press, 1979). Out of the last came the Office of Scholarly Communication and Technology of the ACLS and its newsletter, *Scholarly Communication: Notes on Publishing, Library Trends, and Research in the Humanities*, both of which were discontinued in mid-1987. A useful publication of the now defunct ACLS Office of Scholarly Communication and Technology is Herbert C. Morton et al., *Writings on Scholarly Communication: An Annotated Bibliography of Books and Articles on Publishing, Libraries, Scholarly Research, and Related Issues* (Washington, D.C.: American Council of Learned Societies, 1988).

Apart from these works, most other major (non-history) books on university research and higher education published during the past twenty years or so have failed either to deal seriously with libraries or to demonstrate sophisticated understanding of what they are about. See, for example, Jacques Barzun, *The American University: How It Runs, Where It Is Going* (New York: Harper & Row, 1968), which alludes to libraries in relation to research but does not elaborate; Bernard Berelson, *Graduate Education in the United States* (New York: McGraw-Hill, 1960); Derek Bok, *Beyond the Ivory Tower: Social Responsibilities of the Modern University* (Cambridge, MA: Harvard University Press, 1982); Christopher Jencks and David Riesman, *The Academic Revolution* (New York: Doubleday, 1968); Jaroslav Pelikan, *Scholarship and Its Survival: Questions on the Idea of Graduate Education* (Lawrenceville, NJ: Carnegie Foundation for the Advancement of Learning, 1983). The extensive series of studies by major scholars sponsored by the Carnegie Commission on Higher Education in the 1970s includes works on virtually every aspect of higher education but libraries, which were undergoing virtually as much a revolution as their parent institutions, and which had grown into complex systems. Logan Wilson's important study, *Academics: Then and Now*, published in 1979, omits any mention of librarians, though by then nearly half the universities in the ARL had bestowed formal faculty status on professional librarians. On the latter point see Thomas G. English, "Librarian Status in the Eighty-Nine U.S. Academic Institutions of the Association of Research Libraries: 1982," *College & Research Libraries* 44 (May 1983): 199–211; "Statement of Faculty Status of College and University Librarians," drafted by a committee from Association of College and Research Libraries (ACRL), Association of American Colleges (AAC), and American Association of University Professors (AAUP), *College & Research Libraries News* (Feb. 1974):26. The latter statement was endorsed by the AAUP in 1972; see "Organizations Endorsing the Statement on Faculty Status," *College & Research Libraries News* (May 1974): 109.

The two recent best-selling jeremiads, Allan Bloom's *The Closing of the American Mind* (New York: Simon & Schuster, 1987) and *Cultural Literacy*, by E. D. Hirsch, Jr. (Boston: Houghton, Mifflin, 1987), both passionately concerned with ideas and reading, contain no references to libraries. In her recent *Humanities in America: A Report to the President, the Congress, and the American People* (Washington, D.C., 1988), Lynne V. Cheney, chairman of the National Endowment for the Humanities, criticizes the treatment of the humanities in higher education. Cheney refers to humanities-oriented programs and activities in public nonacademic agencies, including libraries, as constituting a "parallel school," but she does not deal with the role of libraries in colleges and universities.

7. Two summaries of the conference (which I attended) are Susan Brandehoff, "A Meeting of Minds," *American Libraries* 18 (June 1987): 443–445, and Patricia Senn Breivik, "Making the Most of Libraries in the Search for Academic Excellence," *Change* 19 (July–August 1987): 44–52. The conference background papers were published as *Libraries and the Search for Academic Excellence*, ed. Patricia S. Breivik and R. Wedgeworth (Metuchen, NJ: Scarecrow Press, 1988). The conference was in part sparked by two influential reports on higher education: Ernest L. Boyer, *College: The Undergraduate Experience in America* (New York: Harper & Row, 1987), and Frank Newman, *Higher Education and the American Resurgence* (Princeton, NJ: Carnegie Foundation for the Advancement of Teaching, 1985).

Both of these books discuss briefly problems of library use and the information "explosion."

8. John Higham, "The Matrix of Specialization," in *The Organization of Knowledge in Modern America, 1860–1920,* ed. Alexandra Oleson and John Voss (Baltimore: Johns Hopkins University Press, 1979) 3. The volume includes an article on libraries, John Y. Cole's "Storehouses and Workshops: American Libraries and the Uses of Knowledge," (364–85). A companion volume, *The Pursuit of Knowledge in the Early American Republic: American Scientific and Learned Societies from Colonial Times to the Civil War,* ed. Alexandra Oleson and Sanborn C. Brown (Baltimore: Johns Hopkins University Press, 1976) contains scattered material on books and libraries.

9. The following historical works, for example, contain little or no mention of libraries: Margaret Clapp, ed., *The Modern University* (1950; Hamden CT: Archon Books, 1968); Joseph Ben-David, *American Higher Education: Directions Old and New* (New York: McGraw-Hill, 1972); Joseph Ben-David, *Centers of Learning: Britain, France, Germany, United States* (New York: McGraw-Hill, 1977); David D. Henry, *Challenges Past, Challenges Present: An Analysis of American Higher Education Since 1930* (San Francisco: Jossey-Bass, 1975); Jurgen Herbst, *The German Historical School in American Scholarship: A Study in the Transfer of Culture* (Ithaca, NY: Cornell University Press, 1965); Richard Hofstadter and C. DeWitt Hardy, *The Development and Scope of Higher Education in the United States* (New York: Columbia University Press, 1952); John Higham and Paul K. Conkin, eds., *New Directions in American Intellectual History* (Baltimore: Johns Hopkins University Press, 1979); Richard J. Storr, *The Beginning of the Future: A Historical Approach to Graduate Education in the Arts and Sciences* (New York: McGraw-Hill, 1973); the historical sections in Berelson, *Graduate Education* and in Jencks and Riesman, *Academic Revolution,* cited above in note 6. Hofstadter and Smith's *American Higher Education* contains one document directly related to libraries, the Ticknor letter to Stephen Higginson. Books in which there is brief attention to library resources and services or librarians include the following: Burton J. Bledstein, *The Culture of Professionalism: The Middle Class and the Development of Higher Education in America* (New York: W. W. Norton, 1976); Peter Dobkin Hall, *The Organization of American Culture, 1700–1900: Private Institutions, Elites, and the Origins of American Nationality* (New York: New York University Press, 1982); Frederick Rudolph, *The American College and University: A History* (1962; New York: Vintage Books, 1965); Frederick Rudolph, *Curriculum: A History of the American Undergraduate Course of Study since 1636* (1977; San Francisco: Jossey-Bass, 1978); Richard J. Storr, *The Beginnings of Graduate Education in America* (Chicago: University of Chicago Press, 1953); Laurence R. Veysey, *The Emergence of the American University* (Chicago: University of Chicago Press, 1965).

More thoughtful and direct consideration of libraries can be found in the following works: Arthur E. Bestor, Jr., "The Transformation of American Scholarship," *Library Quarterly* 23 (July 1953): 164–179; John S. Brubacher and Willis Rudy, *Higher Education in Transition: A History of American Colleges and Universities, 1636–1976* 3rd ed. (New York: Harper & Row, 1976) 97–99, 187–88, 283, 367, 413; Robert V. Bruce, *The Launching of Modern American Science, 1846–1876* (New York: Knopf, 1987), which gives a good deal of attention to the effect on scientific development of access to books, or more often lack of such access; Lawrence A. Cremin,

American Education: The National Experience, 1783–1876 (New York: Harper & Row, 1980); Lawrence A. Cremin, *American Education: The Metropolitan Experience, 1876–1980* (New York: Harper & Row, 1988); Roger Geiger, *To Advance Knowledge: The Growth of American Research Universities, 1900–1940* (New York: Oxford University Press, 1986). An essay in *The American Scholar* (Spring 1987), "Libraries and Learning," by Oscar Handlin, is a rare reflection on the subject by a historian, who notes the indifference of scholars to their own university libraries' problems (205–18).

10. Thomas Bender, *New York Intellect: A History of Intellectual Life in New York City, from 1750 to the Beginnings of Our Own Time* (New York: Knopf, 1987) 4–5.

11. Thomas Bender, "The Cultures of Intellectual Life: The City and the Professions," in *New Directions in American Intellectual History* 182; also Thomas Bender, "The Erosion of Public Culture: Cities, Discourses, and Professional Discipline," in *The Authority of Experts: Studies in History and Theory*, ed. Thomas L. Haskell (Bloomington: Indiana University Press, 1984) 84–106.

12. Two recent addresses by presidents of historical associations discuss the impact of such specialization and the need for more synthesis: Thomas Bender, "Wholes and Parts: The Need for Synthesis in American History," *Journal of American History* 73 (June 1986): 120–136 (Organization of American Historians); Carl N. Degler, "In Pursuit of an American History," *American Historical Review* 92 (Feb. 1987): 1–12 (American Historical Association). See also a discussion of a questionnaire circulated among subscribers to the *Journal of American History*, who overwhelmingly expressed the same concern about overspecialization: David Thelen, "The Profession and the *Journal of American History*," *Journal of American History* 73 (June 1986): 9–14.

13. Bender, *New York Intellect* 164.

14. Bailyn, in his classic bibliographic essay *Education in the Forming of American Society: Needs and Opportunities for Study* (1960; New York: W. W. Norton, 1972) defines education "not only as formal pedagogy but as the entire process by which a culture transmits itself across the generations" (14). Cremin's definition is only slightly less broad: "the deliberate, systematic, and sustained effort to transmit, evoke, or acquire knowledge, attitudes, values, skills, or sensibilities, as well as any learning that results from the effort, direct or indirect, intended or unintended." Lawrence A. Cremin, *American Education: The National Experience* ix; see also his *Public Education*, John Dewey Society Lecture no. 15 (New York: Basic Books, 1976) 27.

15. I. R. Willison, *On the History of Libraries and Scholarship; a Paper Presented before the Library History Round Table of the American Library Association, June 26, 1979* (Washington, D.C.: Library of Congress, 1980) 7; see also John P. Feather and David McKitterick, *The History of Books and Libraries: Two Views* (Washington, D.C.: Library of Congress, 1986).

16. Quoted from Fisher Ames, *Works*, ed. Seth Ames (Boston, 1854) 2: 440, in Jesse H. Shera, *Foundations of the Public Library: The Origins of the Public Library Movement in New England, 1629–1855* (Chicago: University of Chicago Press, 1949) 208.

17. Both quoted in Bruce, *Launching of Modern American Science* 50, 38; see also 38–39, 43, 45, 47, 54, 55 on other scientists' lamentations in antebellum America about lack of books for their work.

18. For the origins of the Boston Public Library and Ticknor and Everett's role therein, the classic source is Shera, *Foundations of the Public Library*; a standard history of the Boston Public Library is Walter Muir Whitehill, *Boston Public Library: A Centennial History* (Cambridge, MA: Harvard University Press, 1956). On the origins and history of the Astor Library see Phyllis Dain, *The New York Public Library: A History of Its Founding and Early Years* (New York: New York Public Library, 1972) 3-10; and Harry Miller Lydenberg, *History of the New York Public Library, Astor, Lenox and Tilden Foundations* (New York: New York Public Library, 1923), chap. 2. On Cogswell, Ticknor, Everett, and American education see James McLachlan, *American Boarding Schools: A Historical Study* (New York: Charles Scribner's Sons, 1970) 30-34, 45-101; Storr, *Beginnings of Graduate Education* 15-24, 46-53; Hofstadter and Smith, *American Higher Education* 1:251-52, 255-66; Russel Blaine Nye, *The Cultural Life of the New Nation, 1776-1830* (New York: Harper & Row, 1960) 166, 184, 191-92, 235-37. Everett, who was from 1846 to 1849 president of Harvard, was the first American to earn a Ph.D. degree from Göttingen. Peter Dobkin Hall, in *The Organization of American Culture* (2-4, 108-124), asserts that nineteenth-century New Englanders tended to form private corporations for benevolent purposes, and that libraries were among the "privately-controlled institutions" that before the Civil War exemplified Boston's "tight, seemingly exclusive institutional pattern." This is accurate for the Boston Athenaeum but not the Boston Public Library, which was founded in part in response to the Athenaeum's elitism, and which constituted an innovative mix of public and private auspices, control, and funding. New York State, Hall says, was in its laws less sympathetic than New England to private corporations for charitable purposes. A more recent study of the matter concludes that New York State law was in fact more restrictive in relation to charitable trusts until 1893, but that there was a measure of compensation in the liberal interpretations of incorporation of charitable enterprises. See Stanley N. Katz, Barry Sullivan, and C. Paul Beach, "Legal Change and Legal Autonomy: Charitable Trusts in New York, 1777-1893," *Law and History Review* 4 (Spring 1985): 51-89. Be that as it may, in the library field it was in the public sector that New York lagged; by the 1850s the publicly funded district school library system founded in 1835 was in a moribund condition, its library laws were weak, and the state's largest cities were quite late in establishing public libraries.

It is interesting that in 1855, just after the Astor Library opened, Henry P. Tappan, president of the University of Michigan and a former New York educator, began a movement in New York City to found a great university there, with Astor Library funds, as the apex of a pyramid of learned institutions and societies, including the Astor Library. To put it simply and simplistically, the time was not ripe for such a project and in any case John Jacob Astor's son, William B. Astor, preferred to support and strengthen the Astor Library (Bender, *New York Intellect* 107-114; Storr, *Beginnings of Graduate Education* 82-93).

19. John Y. Cole, "Ainsworth Rand Spofford, The Valiant and Persistent Librarian of Congress," *Librarians of Congress, 1802-1974* (Washington, D.C.: Library of Congress, 1977) 119-41, assesses Spofford's role.

20. Fairly recent relevant publications on academic libraries are: Howard Clayton, "The American College Library: 1800-1860," *Journal of Library History* 3 (April 1968): 120-137; Arthur Hamlin, *The University Library in the United States:*

Its Origins and Development (Philadelphia: University of Pennsylvania Press, 1981), which is more discursive than analytical; *Libraries for Teaching, Libraries for Research* (Chicago: American Library Association, 1977), articles originally appearing in *College & Research Libraries* 37 (1976); Orvin Lee Shiflett, *Origins of American Academic Librarianship* (Norwood, NJ: Ablex, 1981). On academic library collections in particular see also articles by Edward Holley and by Hendrik Edelman and G. Marvin Tatum, Jr. in *Libraries for Teaching*; Erle Hilgert, "Calvin Ellis Stowe: Pioneer Librarian of the Old West," *Library Quarterly* 50 (July 1980): 324–51; Joe W. Kraus, "The Book Collections of Early American College Libraries," *Library Quarterly* 43 (April 1973): 142–59; Louis B. Wright, *Culture on the Moving Frontier* (Bloomington: Indiana University Press, 1955) 62, 72–73. Older general works on academic library history are: Kenneth Brough, *Scholar's Workshop: Evolving Conceptions of Library Service* (Urbana: University of Illinois Press, 1953) and Louis Shores, *Origins of the American College Library, 1638–1800* (New York: Barnes & Noble, 1935). A doctoral dissertation in progress at the School of Library Service, Columbia University (Louis Pisha, "Library Collections at Harvard, Yale, and Brown from the 1780s to the 1870s") will examine the nature of these collections and their relationships to curriculum, intellectual trends, surrounding libraries, and faculty interests.

21. James McLachlan, "The *Choice of Hercules*: American Student Societies in the Early 19th Century," in *The University in Society: Europe, Scotland, and the United States from the 16th to the 20th Century*, ed. Lawrence Stone (Princeton, NJ: Princeton University Press, 1974) 2:493. Also on the libraries of the student societies, see Bruce, *Launching of Modern American Science* 88; Rudolph, *Curriculum* 96–98; Lowell Simpson, "The Development and Scope of Undergraduate Literary Society Libraries at Columbia, Dartmouth, Princeton, and Yale, 1783–1830," *Journal of Library History* 12 (Summer 1977): 209–21.

22. William Landram Williamson, *William Frederick Poole and the Modern Library Movement* (New York: Columbia University Press, 1963) 3–13.

23. U.S. Bureau of Education, *Public Libraries in the United States of America: Their History, Condition, and Management; Special Report*, part 1 (Washington, D.C.: Government Printing Office, 1876).

24. Edward G. Holley, "Academic Libraries in 1876," *College & Research Libraries* 37 (Jan. 1976): 43.

25. Theodore Gill, "Scientific Libraries in the United States," in U.S. Bureau of Education, *Public Libraries in the United States* 183–84, 188–214; see also John L. Thornton and R.I.J. Tully, *Scientific Books, Libraries and Collectors: A Study of Bibliography and the Book trade in Relation to Science*, 3d ed. (London: Library Association, 1971), chap. 10.

26. Phyllis Dain, "Billings, John Shaw," *Dictionary of American Library Biography*, ed. Bohdan S. Wynar (Littleton, CO: Libraries Unlimited, 1978) 26–27. The *Index-Catalogue* was issued in specimen form in 1876; the first full series (16 vols.) was published in 1880–95; the *Index Medicus* was begun in 1879.

27. New York Public Library, *Memorial Meeting in Honor of the Late Dr. John Shaw Billings, April 25, 1913* (New York: 1913) 10.

28. John Higham, "The Matrix of Specialization" 12–16. See also Geiger, *To Advance Knowledge*, on diversification and decentralization of science and scholarship (30 ff.).

29. As the first Director (1896–1913) of the New York Public Library, Billings tried, in his characteristically pragmatic way, to create in effect a "total" system there. He devised a new classification scheme for the holdings; a new card catalog was developed that included indexing of serial publications, something that most libraries by then did not do but which was quite useful at a time when published indexes, especially to scholarly and foreign publications, were still uncommon. Books could not be taken out of the library building, but access to them within was made quick and easy; substantial groups of standard books and reference works were removed from the stacks to open shelves; a publishing program concentrated on bibliographic information. See Dain, *New York Public Library*, chaps. 4, 10. In the nineteenth century a number of American libraries published printed catalogs in book form, which, depending on the quality and quantity of holdings, would serve as valuable bibliographies; but by the end of the century a new technology, the card catalog, which was not easily reproducible, supplanted the printed book. It was not until the advent of another technology, photo offset printing, that printed catalogs again became feasible in the mid-twentieth century, with the most significant publication of that sort being the first Library of Congress *Catalog of Books Represented by Library of Congress Printed Cards*, printed in 167 volumes in 1942–46. Both the British Museum and the Bibliothèque Nationale had many years earlier begun to issue their catalogs in letterpress printed books, a long and tortuous process, albeit the results were quite valuable bibliographically. The Library of Congress until 1942 distributed bibliographic information about its holdings primarily by printing and selling its catalog cards and depositing them in selected large libraries, although of course the Library did publish valuable specialized bibliographies through the years.

30. James R. Beniger, *The Control Revolution: Technological and Economic Origins of the Information Society* (Cambridge, MA: Harvard University Press, 1986) 394. In a doctoral dissertation in progress at the Columbia University School of Library Service on two major suppliers of library and office technology, the Library Bureau and Gaylord Brothers, Gerri Flanzraich has been discovering material that bears out this thesis.

31. Jencks and Riesman, *The Academic Revolution*.

32. On collections see, for example: Robert B. Downs, "The Growth of Research Collections," *Library Trends* 25 (July 1976): 55–80; Robert B. Downs, "Library Resources in the United States," *College & Research Libraries* 35 (Mar. 1974): 97–108; Hendrik Edelman and G. Marvin Tatum, Jr., "The Development of Collections in American University Libraries," *College & Research Libraries* 37 (May 1976): 222–45; Steven Leach, "The Growth Rates of Major Academic Libraries: Rider and Purdue Reviewed," *College & Research Libraries* 37 (Nov. 1976): 531–42; "The Library," in U.S. Office of Education, *Survey of Land-Grant Colleges and Universities*, directed by Arthur J. Klein (Washington, D.C.: Government Printing Office, 1930) 1:609–714; U.S. National Resources Committee, Science Committee, *Research—A National Resource; I, Relation of the Federal Government to Research* (Washington, D.C.: U.S. Government Printing Office, 1938) 179; Jerrold Orne, ed., "Current Trends in Collection Development in University Libraries," *Library Trends* 15 (Oct. 1966); Louis Round Wilson, *The Geography of Reading: A Study of the Distribution and Status of Libraries in the United States* (Chicago: American Library Association, 1938), chap. 5; George Alan Works, *College and University*

Library Problems: A Study of a Selected Group of Institutions Prepared for the Association of American Universities (Chicago: American Library Association, 1927). On buildings see Walter C. Allen, "Library Buildings," *Library Trends* 25 (July 1976): 89–112; David Kaser, "The American Academic Library Building, 1870–1890," *Journal of Library History* 21 (Winter 1986): 60–71; Jerrold Orne, "Academic Library Buildings: A Century in Review," *College & Research Libraries* 37 (July 1976): 316–31. David Kaser is preparing a monograph on the evolution of American library buildings. See Kaser, "19th-Century Academic Library Buildings: A Checklist and Request for an Update," *College & Research Libraries News* 48 (Sept. 1987): 476–78.

33. Edward Shils, "The Order of Learning in the United States: The Ascendancy of the University," in *The Organization of Knowledge in Modern America*, ed. Oleson and Voss, 19.

34. Rudolph, *American College and University* 348.

35. Veysey, *Emergence of the American University* 178; Geiger, *To Advance Knowledge* 86.

36. Quoted from Eliot, *Educational Reform: Essays and Addresses*, ed. David Andrew Weaver (Alton, IL: Shurtleff College Press, 1950) 225, in Hugh Hawkins, "University Identity: The Teaching and Research Functions," in *Organization of Knowledge in Modern America* 288.

37. Geiger, *To Advance Knowledge* 9.

38. Historians were often much concerned with the library (and a number of librarians have been historians). See Raymond Cunningham, "Historian among the Librarians: Herbert Baxter Adams and Modern Librarianship," *Journal of Library History* 21 (Fall 1986): 704–22; John W. Burgess, *Reminiscences of an American Scholar: The Beginnings of Columbia University* (1934; New York: AMS Press, 1966), chaps. 6–7; William Bentinck-Smith, *Building a Great Library: The Coolidge Years at Harvard* (Cambridge, MA: Harvard University Press, 1976). On the other hand, although Berkeley's first full-time librarian (1875–1919), Joseph Cummings Rowell, had been a lecturer in English history, the leading members of the university's influential library committee, set up in 1901, came from varied fields, including the sciences. See Kenneth G. Peterson, *The University of California Library at Berkeley, 1900–1945* (Berkeley: University of California Press, 1970) 43, 74–79. The same was true of the powerful University Senate Library Committee at the University of Illinois, though the history department was quite active in library development. At Illinois, after 1900 the library grew from an inconspicuous place on the American library scene to one of national importance as a result of conscious development by the university's administration working in close collaboration with faculty members and librarians. The Illinois library collections and services improved most rapidly and consistently in subject fields with the most scholarly activity. It was the most productive scholars who had the greatest influence in shaping library growth and on a sustained basis. (Wayne S. Yenawine, "The Influence of Scholars on Research Library Development at the University of Illinois," Ph.D. diss., University of Illinois, 1955.) Winifred Linderman, in "History of the Columbia University Library, 1876–1926," Ph.D. diss., Columbia University, 1959, concludes that improvement in the collections (which were sporadically developed) occurred most rapidly and systematically when there was leadership from the university librarian or departmental librarians, and in "subject fields where there was distinguished activity and faculty interest" (552).

39. Bender, "The Cultures of Intellectual Life" 182. An influential work on the history of higher education and professionalism is Burton J. Bledstein, *The Culture of Professionalism: The Middle Class and the Development of Higher Education in America* (New York: W. W. Norton, 1976). My discussion of the academic librarian's role has been informed by the comments of Bledstein on the abridged version of this paper that was delivered at the Library of Congress conference in 1987.

40. English, "Librarian Status in the Eighty-Nine U.S. Academic Institutions of the Association of Research Libraries," *College & Research Libraries* 44 (May 1983): 199-211; "Statement on Faculty Status of College and University Librarians," *College & Research Libraries News* (Feb. 1974): 26; "Organizations Endorsing the Statement on Faculty Status," *College & Research Libraries News* (May 1974): 109; "Standards for Faculty Status for College and University Librarians," *College & Research Libraries News* (May 1974): 112; Emily Werrell and Laura Sullivan, "Faculty Status for Academic Librarians: A Review of the Literature," *College & Research Libraries* 48 (March 1987): 95-103. Of the nearly half of ARL member libraries whose librarians have faculty status, most are public institutions. How faculty status has actually worked out has not been studied qualitatively; John Brewster Smith, Director of Libraries at the State University of New York at Stony Brook, is currently doing case studies of this phenomenon at two New York State public universities and one private university, as a doctoral dissertation at the School of Library Service, Columbia University.

41. Shiflett, *Origins of American Academic Librarianship*.

42. Veysey notes that at Harvard, President Eliot would take ideologically controversial faculty members from the classroom and assign them to the library (*Emergence of the American University* 97).

43. Works, *College and University Library Problems* 80-83.

44. Joanne Passet Bailey, "'The Rule Rather Than the Exception': Midwest Women as Academic Librarians, 1875-1900," *Journal of Library History* 21 (Fall 1986): 673-96; Hamlin, *University Library* 117-19, 131-32; William J. Cohn, "An Overview of ARL Directors, 1933-1973," *College & Research Libraries* 37 (March 1976): 142-43; Betty Jo Irvine, "Women in Academic-Library, Higher-Education, and Corporate Management: A Research Review," in *The Status of Women in Librarianship: Historical, Sociological, and Economic Issues*, ed. Kathleen M. Heim (New York: Neal-Schuman Publishers, 1983) 288-89; Betty Jo Irvine, "Differences by Sex: Academic Administrators," *Library Trends* 34 (Fall 1985): 235-57; Barbara B. Moran, "The Impact of Affirmative Action on Academic Libraries," *Library Trends* 34 (Fall 1985):199-217; American Library Association, Office for Library Personnel Resources, *Academic and Public Librarians: Data by Race, Ethnicity and Sex* (Chicago: American Library Association, 1986).

45. Shiflett, *Origins of American Academic Librarianship* 275. See also 271-77.

46. *Leaders in American Academic Librarianship: 1925-1975*, ed. Wayne A. Wiegand (Pittsburgh, PA: Beta Phi Mu, 1983). The two major new academic library associations were the Association of College and Reference Libraries (now the Association of College and Research Libraries), which was founded in 1938 under the umbrella of the ALA, and the Association of Research Libraries, a selective institutional membership organization, founded in 1932. Before these two associations were established, there were ALA committees that dealt with academic library concerns, but academic librarians found them insufficient to deal with their

needs. As early as 1904 a number of librarians with scholarly interests, unhappy with the domination of ALA by public librarians, broke away to form the Bibliographic Society of America. See Frank M. McGowan, "The Association of Research Libraries, 1932–1962," Ph.D. diss., University of Pittsburgh, 1972; Charles Edward Hale, "The Origin and Development of the Association of College and Research Libraries, 1889–1960," Ph.D. diss., Indiana University, 1976; Edward G. Holley, "Charles Harvey Brown," in *Leaders in American Academic Librarianship* 29–30; Wayne A. Wiegand, "Library Politics and the Organization of the Bibliographical Society of America," *Journal of Library History* 21 (Winter 1986): 131–57. The Special Libraries Association was established in 1909 for similar reasons. Wayne A. Wiegand, in *The Politics of an Emerging Profession: The American Library Association, 1876–1917* (Westport, CT: Greenwood Press, 1986), documents the growing specialization as well as professionalization within librarianship.

47. The definition of the "universal research library," by Christian Gottlöb Heyne (1810), longtime chief of the university library at Göttingen, is in David McKitterick, *Cambridge University Library: A History: The Eighteenth and Nineteenth Centuries* (Cambridge: Cambridge University Press, 1986) 19–20 (quoted from B. Fabian, "An Eighteenth-Century Research Collection; English Books at Göttingen University Library," *The Library* 1 [1979]: 209–24). See also Philip John Weimerskirch, "Antonio Panizzi and the British Museum Library," in *1981 Bookman's Yearbook*, a study of Panizzi's collecting policies and practices; Edelman and Tatum, "The Development of Collections" 223–26, whose discussion of models is somewhat cursory; Hugo Kunoff, *The Foundations of the German Academic Library* (Chicago: American Library Association, 1982).

48. Geiger, *To Advance Knowledge* 9–10.

49. The standard historical work on reference services is Samuel Rothstein, *The Development of Reference Services through Academic Traditions, Public Library Practices, and Special Librarianship*, ACRL Monographs no. 14 (1955; Boston: Gregg Press, 1972). See also John Neal Waddell, "The Career of Isadore G. Mudge: A Chapter in the History of Reference Librarianship," D.L.S. diss., Columbia University, 1973, and Stanley McElderry, "Readers and Resources: Public Services in Academic and Research Libraries, 1876–1976," *College & Research Libraries* 37 (Sept. 1976): 408–20.

50. Redmond Kathleen Molz, *National Planning for Library Service, 1935–1975* (Chicago: American Library Association, 1984), chaps. 1–2; Works; *College and University Library Problems*, chap. 3.

51. An amusing footnote in this connection (amusing to us, that is, in the 1980s) is provided by Robin Winks in *Cloak & Gown, 1939–1961: Scholars in the Secret War* (New York: William Morrow, 1987), chap. 3. He reveals that Yale's Sterling Library, unknown to the librarians and to the university's president, served as a cover for an Office of Strategic Services operation during World War II. Other research libraries, hearing about the plan to send a faculty member to a neutral capital ostensibly to gather research publications, wanted to join and a cooperative venture was set up, one that was largely bogus and ended in a tangled financial mess.

52. Charles B. Osburn, *Academic Research and Library Resources: Changing Patterns in America* (Westport, CT: Greenwood Press, 1979).

53. Thomas F. O'Connor, "Collection Development in the Yale University Library, 1865-1931," *Journal of Library History* 22 (Spring 1987): 164-89; Thomas F. O'Connor, "The Yale University Library, 1865-1931," D.L.S. diss., Columbia University, 1984.

54. Yenawine, "The Influence of Scholars on Research Library Development at the University of Illinois."

55. Edelman and Tatum, "The Development of Collections" 225; J. Periam Danton, "University Library Book Budgets, 1860, 1910 and 1960," *Library Quarterly* 57 (July 1987): 284-302; also Danton, "University Library Book Budgets, 1860, 1910, and 1960: Introduction to an Inquiry," *Library Quarterly* 53 (July 1983); 384-93. Louis Pisha's dissertation, when completed, will tell us in detail of the collections of Harvard, Yale, and Brown from the 1780s to the 1870s, and in relation to curricular and faculty interests. His findings so far indicate that these collections, while not insubstantial in the American context and in a few fields quite comprehensive, were as a whole hardly of the magnitude to support scholarship except perhaps in a very few fields, despite some recognition of the need to do so, and that they were not well coordinated with curricula. Collecting tended to be uneven and erratic, so that there were strengths and weaknesses varying with time.

56. Geiger, *To Advance Knowledge* 228-29, 233.

57. Dependence on gifts for capital and other research needs was characteristic of the private research universities (Geiger, *To Advance Knowledge* 77-93). Even at Berkeley, where there was steady attention to collecting and a stream of public funds, gifts and endowments were still important to successful collection development (Peterson, *University of California Library* 6-8, 15, 23-33, 178). At Illinois, where the major method of acquisition was through purchase, library resources were "significantly enlarged" by gifts and exchanges (Yenawine, "The Influence of Scholars on Research Library Development at the University of Illinois" 208, 210, 211). Linderman's "History of the Columbia University Library, 1876-1926" documents the importance of gifts to Columbia and the rather uneven development of collections under a succession of chief librarians of varying quality.

58. Works, *College and University Library Problems*; U.S. Office of Education, *Survey of Land-Grant Colleges and Universities*, 649-65, 699-714. Wilson, *The Geography of Reading* 118-25, 133-37.

59. The report went on: the library "is the heart of its scholarly life and no institution of distinguished scholarship can be built around a poor library. A poor library never attracts distinguished scholars. Many faculties would do well to educate their president and trustees in the vital necessity of a good library and especially in the importance of the best library staff and service . . . It seems certain that many institutions committed to a research program could save money by spending more generously on their libraries." (U.S. National Resources Committee, Science Committee, *Research—A National Resource* 179).

60. Samuel Rothstein, "Service to Academia," in *A Century of Service: Librarianship in the United States and Canada*, ed. Sidney L. Jackson, E. B. Herling, E. J. Josey (Chicago: American Library Association, 1976) 84; Edelman and Tatum, "The Development of Collections" 225-26. J. Periam Danton, *Book Selection and Collections: A Comparison of German and American University Libraries* (New York: Columbia University Press, 1963) has thoughtful discussions of the issues of completeness, selection, and faculty versus librarian roles.

61. Arthur Bestor, in a rare mention of the issue by a historian, wrote in 1953: "A fascinating chapter of intellectual history could be written about the philosophical presuppositions and the attitudes toward knowledge, its uses, and its inner relationships that are revealed in the development of schemes like these for the classification of books" ("The Transformation of American Scholarship" 176).

62. An exemplary discussion of this process is Roger S. Bagnall and Carolyn L. Harris, "Involving Scholars in the Preservation Decisions: The Case of the Classicists," *Journal of Academic Librarianship* 13 (July 1987): 140-46.

63. I am indebted for this formulation to the remarks of Maurice F. Tauber, late Melvil Dewey Professor at the Columbia University School of Library Service, in doctoral seminars in the late 1950s.

64. Evelyn Geller, *Forbidden Books in American Public Libraries, 1876-1939: A Study in Cultural Change* (Westport, CT: Greenwood Press, 1984); Wayne A. Wiegand, *"An Active Instrument for Propaganda": The American Public Library during World War I* (Westport, CT: Greenwood Press, 1989), chap. 5; Arthur P. Young, *Books for Sammies: The American Library Association and World War I* (Pittsburgh, PA: Beta Phi Mu, 1981) 47, 52-55; Frederick J. Stielow, "Censorship in the Early Professionalization of American Libraries, 1876 to 1929," *Journal of Library History* 18 (Winter 1983): 37-54.

65. See Walter P. Metzger, *Academic Freedom in the Age of the University* (1955; New York: Columbia University Press, 1961); Carol S. Gruber, *Mars and Minerva: World War I and the Uses of Higher Learning in America* (Baton Rouge: Louisiana State University Press, 1975); Ellen W. Schrecker, *No Ivory Tower: McCarthyism and the Universities* (New York: Oxford University Press, 1986).

66. Peterson, *University of California Library* 16-19.

67. Paul H. Mosher, "Collection Evaluation in Research Libraries: The Search for Equality, Consistency, and System in Collection Development," *Library Resources & Technical Services* 23 (Winter 1979): 20; American Library Association, Collection Development Committee, *Guidelines for Collection Development*, ed. David L. Perkins (Chicago: American Library Association, 1979); Esther Nilsen, "The History of Book Selection Policy in U.S. Academic Libraries from 1876 to the Present," unpublished essay, School of Library Service, Columbia University, 1985.

68. *Leaders in American Academic Librarianship* 226, 242, 352; Danton, *Book Selection and Collections*, chap. 3.

69. Douglas Waples and Harold Lasswell, *National Libraries and Foreign Scholarship (Notes on Recent Selections in Social Science)* (Chicago: University of Chicago Press, 1936). On other comparative studies that include the New York Public Library see Phyllis Dain, "Harry M. Lydenberg and American Library Resources: A Study in Modern Library Leadership." *Library Quarterly* 47 (Oct. 1977): 461-62.

70. A brief history of private independent libraries (for example, Folger, Newberry, Huntington, Linda Hall) is William S. Budington, " 'To Enlarge the Sphere of Human Knowledge': The Role of the Independent Research Library," *College & Research Libraries* 37 (July 1976): 299-315; historical sketches of a number of such libraries, plus one on the Independent Research Libraries Association (founded in 1972), appear in *Research Institutions and Learned Societies*, ed. Joseph C. Kiger, *The Greenwood Encylopedia of American Institutions* vol. 5 (Westport, CT: Greenwood Press, 1982). Gordon Ray, late president of the John Simon Guggenheim Foundation and active in

research library affairs, noted the great importance of independent libraries in supporting original research; in his view they were doing it better but receiving less recognition than universities libraries (*American Libraries as Centers of Scholarship* 17–19, 32–34).

71. The variety and complexity of American public libraries as governmental and corporate structures—and hence the difficulty in defining them, a problem deriving from their variegated history—is discussed and demonstrated at length in Carleton Bruns Joeckel's classic study, *The Government of the American Public Library* (Chicago: The University of Chicago Press, 1935).

72. "College Libraries," in U.S. Bureau of Education, *Public Libraries in the United States* 60, 104.

73. Quincy, "Free Libraries," in U.S. Bureau of Education, *Public Libraries in the United States* 393, 401.

74. A. R. Spofford, "Periodical Literature and Society Publications," in U.S. Bureau of Education, *Public Libraries in the United States* 681–685 and Justin Winsor, "Library Memoranda," 712. A 1988 Columbia University School of Library Service doctoral dissertation dealing with thought and practice among American librarians and libraries regarding physical care and preservation of collections indicates the concern in a number of urban public libraries to retain materials for their archival and historical value (Barbra Higginbotham, "Preservation in American Libraries at the Turn of the Century: A Portrait of Thought and Activity in the Period 1876 to 1910").

75. Williamson, *William Frederick Poole* 81–82, 120, 135; also Gwaldys Spencer, *The Chicago Public Library: Origins and Backgrounds* (Chicago: The University of Chicago Press, 1943) 337, 348–50, 394, 397–402.

76. Lowell A. Martin, *Library Response to Urban Change: A Study of the Chicago Public Library* (Chicago: American Library Association, 1969) 51–58, 64–67, 242–44. Poole, who left the Chicago Public Library in 1887 for the Newberry Library, which he directed until 1894, came to approve of such a division of labor in Chicago, given the establishment of the Newberry and then the Crerar as reference libraries. (Williams, *William Frederick Poole* 89–90, 136, 148–49). Veysey, in *The Emergence of the American University*, notes that at the University of Chicago "adequate library facilities were . . . always missing" (179); Richard J. Storr, in *The Beginnings: A History of the University of Chicago* (Chicago: University of Chicago Press, 1966), does not mention libraries in discussing the founding and early history of the university, possibly because his sources did not. Helen Lefkowitz Horowitz, in *Culture & the City: Cultural Philanthropy in Chicago from the 1880s to 1917* (Lexington, KY: University Press of Kentucky, 1976), discusses the popular character of the Chicago Public Library, and compares it to other more elite institutions in the city (32, 47, 98–99, 103–4, 114, 120–25, 165, 215–16).

77. Quotation from the Minneapolis Public Library annual report (1890), in Bruce Weir Benidt, *The Library Book: Centennial History of the Minneapolis Public Library* (Minneapolis: Minneapolis Public Library and Information Center, 1984) 55; see also 38, 42, 50, 54, 57–64, 71; and on the Countryman era, chap. 3.

78. Frank B. Woodford, *Parnassus on Main Street: A History of the Detroit Public Library* (Detroit: Wayne State University Press, 1965) 398.

79. Arthur P. Young, "Daniel Coit Gilman in the Formative Period of American Librarianship," *Library Quarterly* 45 (April 1975): 132; Philip Arthur Kalisch, *The*

Enoch Pratt Free Library: A Social History (Metuchen, NJ: Scarecrow Press, 1969) 221-24; Cunningham, "Historian among the Librarians." Adams also promoted public libraries in popular education and their use in university extension programs; see Herbert Baxter Adams, "Public Libraries and Popular Education," in University of the State of New York, *Home Education Bulletin* no. 31 (May 1900).

80. Dain, *New York Public Library* 50, 57-61, 70.

81. On the origin, founding, and mission of the New York Public Library see Dain, *New York Public Library*; Dain, "Harry M. Lydenberg"; Lydenberg, *History of the New York Public Library*. For a brief summary of the subsequent problems and direction of the library, a project on which the present author is working, see Phyllis Dain, "New York Public Library, Astor, Lenox and Tilden Foundations," in *Research Institutions and Learned Societies* 387-93.

82. Dain, *New York Public Library* 124-30; Dain, "Harry M. Lydenberg." The range of the library's holdings is described in Karl Brown, *A Guide to the Reference Collections of the New York Public Library* (New York: New York Public Library, 1941); and Sam P. Williams, *Guide to the Research Collections of the New York Public Library* (Chicago: American Library Association, 1975).

83. For example, in 1921, on the heels of the nationwide Red Scare, the Yale University Corporation refused a gift of the extensive Nettlau collection on anarchism in part because of its controversial contents. Yale's president and several members of the Corporation did favor acceptance, and it is fair to say that if Nettlau had not asked that as a condition of his gift he accompany the collection as cataloger, they might have prevailed, even though other members were opposed to acquiring such radical materials, and the Yale librarian, Andrew Keogh, was worried about the controversiality of the collection. It seems that there were no efforts to modify Nettlau's condition, and Yale did not get his collection. (O'Connor, "Yale University Library" 302-7.) On the other hand, Columbia University in 1903 reported acquisition of a "remarkably complete" collection on anarchism (Linderman, "History of the Columbia University Library" 305), which was at that time, soon after the assassination of President McKinley by a self-proclaimed anarchist, a subject considered dangerously radical by the public. The New York Public Library, beginning in 1898, had accepted, with no comment, the Marxist collections of socialist F. A. Sorge, and continued to acquire such materials as well as subscribing to radical periodicals. (Lydenberg, *History of the New York Public Library* 391; also Brown, *Guide* 150-51, and Williams, *Guide* 193-94.)

84. New York Public Library Board of Trustees, Library Committee, Minutes (Feb. 9, 1914), 4:112-114, 116. A statement of the library's policy of balanced collecting is in NYPL, *Report* (1935) 22. See also NYPL, Board of Trustees, Executive Committee, Minutes (March 5, 1937), 39: 35; (Nov. 5, 1948), 50: 96-98; NYPL, Board of Trustees, Minutes (Nov. 10, 1948): 61-62. In 1914 Edwin H. Anderson, the director of the library, rejected a request from a reader for a statement that he was a library user, "the policy of the library forbidding our giving any information about readers or visitors" (Edwin Anderson, letter to Julius Tietze, 12 Oct. 1914 [copy], NYPL Archives, General Library Papers). Spencer points out liberal views in Chicago vis à vis the founding of the Public Library in the 1870s (*Chicago Public Library* 350).

On American public libraries' censorship of pro-German materials during World War I and the position of the NYPL concerning collecting research materials see Wiegand, "*An Active Instrument for Propaganda*," chap. 5. On NYPL policies toward use during World Wars I and II, see NYPL, Board of Trustees, Minutes (Dec. 12, 1917), 13: 201–02,and "Report of Special Investigator" in NYPL, Board of Trustees, Executive Committee, Minutes (Feb. 9, 1940), 42: 47; (April 5, 1940), 42: 91; (May 8, 1942), 44: 96; (Oct. 9, 1942), 44: 143; (Nov. 6, 1942), 44: 202; (Dec. 4, 1942), 44: 223; (June 4, 1943), 45: 125; (Dec. 3, 1943), 45: 220; (Feb. 4, 1944), 46: 22; (May 5, 1944), 46: 83; (June 9, 1944), 46: 100; (May 4, 1945), 47: 79; (Dec. 8, 1944), 47: 184. The NYPL's liberalism concerning collections also did not necessarily extend to library staff. If during World War I the research library tried to get everything it could from whatever source, the trustees and the administration did investigate "alien enemies" among the staff, that is, employees who were "born in Germany or Austria-Hungary and have not become citizens of the United States." Out of ten such employees at the NYPL, three were determined to be "strictly speaking, enemy aliens," two of whom were low level employees in the central building superintendent's division and one in the printing office; the first two were dismissed for "good reasons" [See NYPL, Board of Trustees, Executive Committee, Minutes (Dec. 7, 1917), 19: 309; (Jan. 4, 1918), 20: 12–13]. At other times the library defended the rights of its employees to their personal political opinions. See H. M. Lydenberg, letter to Mildred E. Loomis (copy), 19 April 1912, NYPL Archives, General Library Papers; NYPL, Board of Trustees, Minutes, (Oct. 13, 1949), 45: 50.

85. Dain, "Harry Miller Lydenberg," 460–61; Robert A. Karlowich, "Harry Miller Lydenberg and Soviet Libraries in 1923," Association of College and Research Libraries, Slavic and East European Section, *Newsletter* 3 (1987): 35–44; Phyllis Dain, on Karlowich, et al., *Newsletter* 44–50; Bentinck-Smith, *Building a Great Library* 3–5, 9–15, 18, 108–09, 126–28, 157; Robert Hessen, "Hoover Institution on War, Revolution and Peace," in *Research Institutions and Learned Societies* 271.

86. One cannot demonstrate directly that the trustees were anti-Semitic, though scattered comments to that effect have been found; but it is telling that in a heavily Jewish city like New York, with so many Jewish lawyers, businessmen, professional people, and intellectuals, the first Jewish trustee was elected in 1902 only for political reasons. He remained the sole Jewish member until his death in 1930, after which another Jew replaced him; several years later a second Jewish trustee was elected. Similar observations can be made about Roman Catholics. From the formation of the library in 1895 to 1970, when the board was reorganized, enlarged, and made somewhat more representative, 96 out of the 110 trustees (not including ex-officio members representing the city government), were apparently Protestant; eight appear to have been Roman Catholic, and six Jewish. These figures derive from my own prosopographical studies of the trustees. On the composition of the board see also Dain, *New York Public Library* 78–86, 229–30, 252, 256–57, 260–63; on expressed attitudes toward Jews see 112; 387, n59; 408, n7, n18; 409, n32. On the special nature of the Jewish Division see A. S. Freidus, "The Scope of the Jewish Division in the Light of Library Practices," *Bulletin of the New York Public Library* 18 (Feb. 1914): 104–07. On financial support of the Jewish Division see NYPL, *Report* (1928) 40; NYPL, Board of Trustees, Executive Committee, Minutes, (June 4, 1926), 28: 80–81; (April 8, 1927), 29: 54–55; (June 3, 1927): 85; (June 7, 1928), 30: 94–95; (Nov. 9, 1928), 30: 141, 158–157; (May 3, 1929), 31: 47–48.

87. Marva L. DeLoach and Glenderlyn Johnson, "Afro-American Collections," in *Ethnic Collections in Libraries*, ed. E. J. Josey and Marva L. DeLoach (New York: Neal-Schuman, 1983) 119-49; Elinor Des Verney Sinnette, "Arthur Schomburg, Black Bibliophile and Curator: His Contribution to the Collection and Dissemination of Materials about Africans and Peoples of African Descent," D.L.S. diss., Columbia University, 1977; Roi Ottley and William J. Weatherby, *The Negro in New York: An Informal Social History, 1626-1940* (New York: Praeger, 1967) 250-60; Gilbert Osofsky, *Harlem: The Making of a Ghetto: Negro New York, 1890-1930* (New York: Harper & Row, 1968) 152, 181. Actually the Schomburg Collection was bought for the Division of Negro Literature and History, a reference library established at the 135th Street Branch in 1925 which was later named the Schomburg Collection of Negro Literature (NYPL, *Report* (1925) 67; (1926) 67; (1940) 123).

88. The modern development of the library's music collection can be dated from 1914 and 1915, when the distinguished music critic of the *New York Times*, Richard Aldrich, was brought in as a consultant, and the musicologist Otto Kinkledey was appointed chief of the Music Division (Board of Trustees, Executive Committee, Minutes [Feb. 6, 1914], 16: 61-66; March 5, 1915, 17: 42-46). Kinkeldey, who built the Music Division to its great eminence and later became the first professor of musicology in the United States (at Cornell University) discussed the state of music collections in the United States up to 1937 in a classic article, "Training for Music Librarianship: Aims and Opportunities," in *Reader in Music Librarianship*, ed. Carol June Bradley (Washington, D.C.: Microcard Editions Books, 1973) 299-300. On Kinkeldey see Carol June Bradley, "Kinkeldey, Otto," *Dictionary of American Library Biography*, 286-89.

89. John Shaw Billings, letter to Professor J. E. Spingarn, 21 Dec. 1911 (copy); H. M. Lydenberg, letter to Martha Foote Crow, 14 April 1913 (copy); E. H. Anderson, letter to Rev. Joseph H. McMahon, 9 [?] Oct. 1913 (copy); H. M. Lydenberg, letter to Upton Sinclair, 13 Aug. 1914 (copy), NYPL Archives, General Library Papers; Esther Johnston, "Entrance on Forty-Second Street," *Bulletin of the New York Public Library* 73 (March 1969): 200-201; NYPL, *Report* (1928) 42; Abraham Berger, "The Jewish Division of the New York Public Library," *Jewish Book Annual* 23 (1965/66): 46-47.

90. The social and cultural historian Neil Harris writes that at the end of the nineteenth century, universities, specialized scholars' collections, and the Library of Congress took over the job of "servicing the needs of specialists and academics": the public libraries were left to handle "middle-level inquiries," to satisfy "a thirst for recreation through the reading of fiction," and to serve to some extent as resources for resolving public controversies. ("The Lamps of Learning: Popular Lights and Shadows," in *Organization of Knowledge in Modern America* 434, 436.) Harris is perhaps too sweeping; I do not think that there was such a definitive or absolute or universal shift.

91. The reading rooms at the New York Public Library were jammed by students from the municipal free colleges, Columbia University, and New York University, plus others, to the point where in 1930 college students were barred altogether except under special circumstances, not to return for unlimited use until 1955. Surveys in the 1950s and 1960s still showed heavy use of the research collections by local students and faculty members; the Graduate Center of the new City

University of New York (organized in 1961), without a supporting research library, was located on Forty-second Street, across the street from the New York Public Library . See NYPL, *Report* (1920) 22; (1921) 21; (1922) 26; (1924) 22–24; (1925) 23; (1926) 22; (1929) 24–25; (1930) 24; "The Main Reading Room in the Autumn," *Bulletin of the New York Public Library* 25 (Nov. 1921): 747–49; Keyes D. Metcalf, "Notes on Variation in the Amount and Use of the Reference Department of the New York Public Library," *Bulletin of New York Public Library* 40 (Nov. 1936): 909–10, 915–18, 924–25; *Ten Year Report of the New York Public Library, 1946–1956* (New York: The New York Public Library, 1957) 29–31; Nelson Associates, *User Survey of the New York Public Library Research Libraries* (New York: 1969) 1:4–17, 23–25. One source of the New York Public Library's difficulties was that, because of historical circumstances of its founding and then, among other conditions, financial problems, there was until 1970 no college-level public circulating library collection in Manhattan such as other cities had, at the same time as local college collections were not strong. The Research Libraries therefore had to serve a public much more diverse and numerous than they could support.

Although other cities might not have experienced quite the same pressures, this was for some a perennial problem at times; urban public libraries in the aggregate had as late as 1929/30 considerably larger collections than urban colleges and universities. See Robert T. Grazier, "The Development of the Urban University Library," *Library Trends* 10 (April 1962): 458–68; William M. Randall, *The College Library: A Descriptive Study of the Libraries in Four-year Liberal Arts Colleges in the United States* (Chicago: American Library Association and the University of Chicago Press, 1932). The Detroit Public Library in the 1920s served the College of the City of Detroit (later Wayne State University) as virtually a college library, and Johns Hopkins students heavily used branches of the Enoch Pratt Free Library (Woodford, *Parnassus on Main Street* 241–42; Kalisch, *The Enoch Pratt Free Library* 125). Of course in some places the situation might well have been reversed. In New Haven, for example, community members used Yale's library in the absence of a good public library (O'Connor, "Yale University Library" 434–39), and other universities around the country, private as well as public, had provisions for unaffiliated users, with MIT opening its collections in 1919 to corporations that paid retainer fees (Geiger, *To Advance Knowledge* 178; also Peterson, *The University of California Library* 171–72). The classic analysis of library use studies up to the 1940s is Bernard Berelson, with Lester Asheim, *The Library's Public: A Report of the Public Library Inquiry* (New York: Columbia University Press, 1949).

92. Lee Ash and William G. Miller, *Subject Collections*, 6th ed. (New York: R. R. Bowker Company, 1985) and *American Library Directory*, 41st ed. (New York: R. R. Bowker Company, 1988) indicate the general holdings and numerous special collections in public libraries; see also Rothstein, *Development of Reference Services* 33–34. On services to business and industry see Anthony Thomas Kruzas, *Business and Industrial Libraries in the United States, 1820–1940* (New York: Special Libraries Association, 1965). On legislative reference libraries before World War I see John Boynton Kaiser, *Law, Legislative and Municipal Reference Libraries; An Introductory Manual and Bibliographical Guide* (Boston: Boston Book Company, 1914) 251–59. On the principle of local history collecting, see Arthur F. Bostwick, *The American Public Library*, 3d ed. (New York: D. Appleton, 1928) 77; Joseph L. Wheeler and Herbert Goldhor, *Practical Administration of Public Libraries* (New York: Harper &

Row, 1962) 352–53, 471. In 1983, 278 of the 1,373 U.S. government document depository libraries were public libraries; of these public libraries, sixty-six (23.7 percent) achieved depository status in the nineteenth century, thirty-nine (14 percent) did so between 1900 and 1925, and fifteen (5.4 percent), between 1926 and 1950. Figures derived from Peter Hernon, Charles R. McClure, Gary P. Purcell, *GPO's Depository Library Program: A Descriptive Analysis* (Norwood, NJ: Ablex, 1985) 3, 59, 92–93.

93. *Studies in Creative Partnership: Federal Aid to Public Libraries during the New Deal*, ed. Daniel F. Ring (Metuchen, NJ: Scarecrow Press, 1980); *Union Catalogs in the United States*, ed. Robert B. Downs, (Chicago: American Library Association, 1942).

94. From 1980 to 1982, the *Wilson Library Bulletin* ran a series of articles on major public libraries that discussed this problem, among others: see, for example: Colleen Cayton, "Daring to Be Different: The Denver Public Library," 56 (Mar. 1982): 508–9; Rita Fuerst, "The Born Again Cleveland Public Library," 54 (Feb. 1980): 366–67; Jerrold Hickey, "Boston Public Library: Balancing the Books," 55 (June 1981): 743–49; Philip Lentz, "The Free Library of Philadelphia: Making the Hard Choices," 55 (Sept. 1980): 35–36; Patricia Rice, "St. Louis Public Library: Trying to Remain Necessary," 56 (May 1982): 677. See also *The Public Library in the Urban Setting; the Thirty-Second Conference of the Graduate Library School , July 31–August 2, 1967* (Chicago: The University of Chicago Press, 1968); and *Future of the Main Urban Library; Report of a Conference in Chicago at the Chicago Public Library, October 26–27, 1978*, ed. Paxton P. Price (Las Cruces, NM: Urban Libraries Council, 1978).

2

The Library of Congress and American Scholarship, 1865–1939

John Y. Cole

Although it was established in 1800, the Library of Congress did not emerge as a truly national institution until after the Civil War, or as a useful research library until after the turn of the century. Two men were responsible for these transformations: Ainsworth Rand Spofford, Librarian of Congress from 1865 to 1897, and Herbert Putnam, Librarian from 1899 to 1939.

An expansion-minded nationalist and the Library's greatest collection builder, Spofford spent his thirty-three years as Librarian in increasingly crowded rooms in the U.S. Capitol, and his success as an "accumulator" made a separate library building a necessity. When the doors of the monumental new structure were opened in 1897, it was hailed as "the largest, the costliest, and safest" library building in the world.[1] The new building, strong support from Congress, and enthusiasm among professional librarians for a "national library" presented the Library of Congress with unparalleled opportunities for growth and service to its principal constituencies: Congress, the federal government, authors and publishers, and the general public.

Herbert Putnam, Librarian of Congress from 1899 to 1939, began service to two new constituencies: the nation's libraries and its scholars, or "serious investigators," as Putnam called them. In particular it was Putnam, an experienced librarian, who made "assisting forward the work of scholarship" a major goal of the Library of Congress. In 1939 Putnam was succeeded as Librarian of Congress by writer and poet Archibald MacLeish, who was chosen by President Franklin D. Roosevelt as the kind of nationally known, "scholarly man of letters" the President felt should head the Library.[2]

Between Ainsworth Spofford and Herbert Putnam, from 1865 to 1939, the Library of Congress became one of the world's largest libraries, a unique national institution that identified and brought together common concerns of American government, librarianship, and scholarship. Its book collections grew in number from about 70,000 to more than 6 million volumes, and its manuscripts, maps, music, prints, and photographs were organized into true research collections. And its staff, between 1865 and 1939, grew in number from seven to more than 1,100.[3]

In the same years, however, the Library of Congress also became one of the world's most complicated libraries: a legislative agency with executive functions; a government library open to the public; a national institution "universal" in scope, collecting books and research materials from around the world; and a large bureaucracy serving diverse, often competing constituencies. These varied functions and roles have obscured the Library's substantial contributions to American scholarship, especially in American history, in cartography, in music, and in bibliographic work in several fields. In particular, however, the importance of the Library's cataloging and technical services to the development of cooperative scholarship in America has not been fully understood or appreciated. The librarians, scholars, congressmen, and private citizens who built the Library of Congress into a national institution between 1865 and 1939 helped shape the informal systems of scholarly communication and research support that exist in America today.

BUILDING A NATIONAL COLLECTION, 1865–1899

Cultural nationalism was the primary force behind the early growth of the Library of Congress; today it is still the unifying force between the Library's legislative and national roles. Ainsworth Rand Spofford, the Cincinnati bookman who was appointed Librarian of Congress on the last day of 1864 by President Abraham Lincoln, spent his career pleading with and eventually persuading Congress to view its Library as a national institution. Spofford's assertion that "there is almost no work within the vast range of literature and science which may not at some time prove useful to the legislature of a great nation," echoed Thomas Jefferson's persuasive rationale for selling his personal library to the Congress in 1815: "there is no subject to which a member of Congress may not have occasion to refer."[4] The Jeffersonian concept of universality, the belief that all subjects are important to the Library of the American legislature, is the philosophy and rationale behind the comprehensive collecting policies of today's Library of Congress. Moreover, the broad scope and diversity of the Library's collections has provided each Librarian of Congress with opportunities to develop new collection-based functions or services.[5]

Spofford's national ambitions for the Library of Congress were supported by Joseph Henry, the secretary of the Smithsonian Institution, who felt the Library of Congress, not the Smithsonian, should become this country's great national storehouse of books and knowledge. In 1866 Henry and Spofford transferred the entire Smithsonian Library, consisting of 40,000 volumes, to the Library of Congress. This acquisition, which became the basis of the Library of Congress's collections of science, official foreign documents, and learned journals, also was important because access to the collection by researchers was stipulated by law.

The post-Civil War expansionist mood led to the growth of the federal government and a new importance for the nation's capital. Taking advantage of this trend, as well as his personal friendships with Ohio Congressmen, Spofford built a national institution. His models were the national libraries of Europe, particularly the British Museum Library; he wanted a comprehensive and current collection of national literature. Since the Republic rested "upon the popular intelligence," the library would be open to all, used by Congress and by the American people. The Librarian never hesitated to compare his meager institution to the great libraries of other countries. In 1867, for example, arguing (successfully) for an unprecedented $100,000 appropriation to purchase one of the richest scholarly collections in America, the personal library of archivist Peter Force, Spofford reminded Congress that the largest collection of Americana in the world was in the British Museum Library, not in any American institution.

Spofford's most significant accomplishment was the centralization of all United States copyright deposit and registration activities at the Library of Congress. The copyright law of 1870 ensured the continuing development of the Americana collections, for it stipulated that two copies of every book, pamphlet, map, print, and piece of music registered for copyright be deposited in the Library. Thus a massive, continually growing research collection was born—and the collection itself was without purchase cost. But five years later, the Library's rooms in the west front of the Capitol were overflowing and, in urging a separate Library building, Spofford complained to Congress that he was in the "unhappy predicament of presiding over the greatest chaos in America."[6]

The organization of research collections of maps, music, and prints, all piling up in the Capitol because of the new copyright law, would have to be postponed until the move into the new building. Manuscripts were different, however, and Spofford did not want to wait. He felt that the United States government, through its national library, should collect, preserve, and immediately make available primary source material for the study of American history. In 1875 he asked Congress for funds to employ "a competent historical scholar" to take care of the Library's manuscripts collection, which had come mostly from the Jefferson, Smithsonian, and Peter Force acquisitions.[7] The request was denied, but he had made his point. The new building was not authorized until 1886, but when it finally opened in 1897, a professional historian, Herbert

Friedenwald of the Johns Hopkins University, was hired to head the new manuscripts department.

There were other ways in which Spofford prepared the Library of Congress for the role of a research library. He extended the hours of opening and welcomed the use of the Library by members of the public. And until the 1880s, when the Library's space needs overwhelmed him, he produced book catalogs and even a few bibliographies.

In 1895, on the eve of the move into a new building, Spofford's library had thirty-eight employees. In a reorganization proposal he reminded Congress that the Boston Public Library, with two-thirds as many volumes and no copyright function, had a staff of 140 and that the British Museum Library employed 220. In the "new and splendid home for the Nation's books provided by the far-sighted Congress," he asked for 97 staff positions, plus separate departments for printed books, periodicals, manuscripts, maps and charts, works of art, copyright, cataloging, and binding.[8]

In 1896, Congress held hearings on the Library and its future role. The principal witnesses were Spofford, Melvil Dewey of the New York State Library, and Herbert Putnam, head of the Boston Public Library. Dewey and Putnam, both representing the American Library Association (ALA), advocated a new leadership role for the Library of Congress. They thought it should go beyond Spofford's concept of a great accumulation of national literature and begin to serve other libraries; in fact it should become in Dewey's words, "a center to which the libraries of the whole country can turn for inspiration, guidance, and practical help." Centralized cataloging, interlibrary loan, and a national union catalog were among the services they recommended.[9]

Without addressing this question directly, Congress agreed to expand all phases of the Library's operations in the subsequent reorganization, and increased the size of the staff to 108. Moreover, the authority to set the Library's rules and regulations, which Spofford had assumed decades earlier, was formally transferred from the Joint Congressional Committee on the Library to the Librarian of Congress. The Librarian was to choose the Library's employees "solely with reference to fitness for the particular duties," an action that kept the Library outside the government civil service system. The reorganization, enacted as part of the Library's annual appropriation, also gave the Senate the power to accept or reject the President's nomination of a Librarian of Congress.[10]

In the spring of 1897, President William McKinley nominated a new Librarian, not a library professional as the ALA hoped, but a personal friend, the former diplomat and newspaperman John Russell Young. The seventy-two-year-old Spofford stepped aside to become chief assistant Librarian. Young's concept of a national library was similar to Spofford's: it was to be a comprehensive national collection, open to all who came to Washington to use it. A capable administrator who made several excellent appointments to the Library's staff, Young did a good job in spite of poor health.[11] Unfortunately he died in office in January 1899, after only a year and a half as Librarian. The ALA immediately and forcefully began lobbying President McKinley to nominate an experienced library administrator to head the national library. Their choice was Herbert Putnam of the Boston Public Library. The President agreed, Putnam agreed, and the man who had testified at the 1896 reorganization hearings about the need for the Library of Congress to begin serving other libraries was given the opportunity to implement his ideas.

ORGANIZING KNOWLEDGE FOR PUBLIC SERVICE, 1899–1939

The son of publisher George Palmer Putnam, Herbert Putnam graduated from Harvard in 1883. He attended Harvard University Law School for one year before he received, through a family friend, an offer to become librarian of the Minneapolis Athenaeum. He accepted the job, but also continued his legal studies, and was admitted to the Minnesota bar in 1885. Two years later he presided over the merger of the Athenaeum with the Minneapolis Public Library, and soon impressed everyone with his performance as the first city librarian of Minneapolis. In 1892 he returned to New England, and after practicing law for three years was elected superintendent of the Boston Public Library. In 1899, when he became Librarian of Congress, he was only thirty-seven years old.[12] In 1913 Putnam looked back on his Boston and Washington careers:

At Boston my chief work was in adapting the library to the new building and in popularizing its facilities; in Washington, it has been in the nationalization of the Library of Congress by developing its resources for service to scholarship and by extending the benefits of its collections and of its technical processes to the country at large.[13]

Here is the key to the remarkable achievements of Herbert Putnam between 1899 and 1939: his vision of nationalizing the collections and services of the Library by extending them from Washington to the nation. It was a vision he fulfilled in only three years.

The first experienced librarian to serve as Librarian of Congress, Putnam immediately established a working partnership between the Library and the American library movement. In fact, the Library of Congress soon became the leader among American libraries, a turn of events in accord with Putnam's view, as expressed in the 1896 hearings, of the proper role of a national library. Rather than serving solely as a comprehensive national collection in the capital city, a national library should, he felt, actively serve other libraries. In establishing a systematic program of widespread service to libraries and scholars, Putnam went beyond the Panizzian model that Spofford had followed, even though Putnam and Panizzi were in full accord on another important point: each aspired to build collections from all countries and in all languages.[14]

Putnam explained his new approach in a July 1901 speech at the annual meeting of the ALA, declaring:

If there is any way in which our National Library may "reach out" from Washington, it should reach out. . . . There should be possible also a service to the country at large: a service to be extended through the libraries which are the local centers of research.[15]

Speaking to members of the American Historical Association (AHA) six months later, Putnam explained that a national library was "a collection universal in scope which has a duty to the country as a whole," and its prime duty was to scholarship.[16]

In the quarter-century before Putnam took office, a new structure of scientific and scholarly activity had evolved in the United States. Professional schools and new universities offering graduate work were established; numerous professional associations and societies came into existence; and the federal government became an active supporter of education, research, and scientific activity. By 1900, as Arthur Bestor has pointed out, the age of the great library had arrived in America; its characteristics included huge book stacks, scientific cataloging and classification, and full-time professional staffs.[17] In 1901 the Library of Congress, by then the nation's largest library, also had become part of the new pattern of American intellectual activity, for it had begun to play a decisive role in organizing recorded knowledge for public service.

Putnam's actions in 1901 were imaginative and decisive. They were approved by both the Joint Committee on the Library and professional librarians. The year's innovations included the sale and distribution of printed catalog cards; the first steps in the development of a national union catalog; the publication of the first volume of the Library's new classification scheme; the extension of access to the Library to "scientific investigators and duly qualified individuals throughout the United States"; the inauguration of a national interlibrary loan service; and the publication of listings of the Library's manuscript holdings.

The three-by-five-inch Library of Congress printed card was itself a revolution that encouraged standardized practices, cooperation, and the sharing of information. The sale of the cards for a nominal fee enabled other libraries to use Library of Congress bibliographic data, and to save money by not having to catalog the items themselves. The deposit by the Library of sets of its printed cards in several dozen libraries around the country enabled researchers to discover whether a particular book was in the Library of Congress, the first step in resource sharing. The cards included the new Library of Congress classification numbers, which libraries were free to use. The first classification schedule, *Class E and F: American History and Geography: Preliminary and Provisional Scheme of Classification*, was published in 1901.

The interlibrary loan service established by Putnam in 1901 is a prime example of his fervent belief in extending the Library's usefulness to the country at large. A radical step for the Library of Congress, it signaled the institution's transition from a national storehouse of books to a national laboratory or workshop for promoting the use of its collections. In 1905, the Librarian explained his philosophy and how the new service worked. The books sent outside the Library, he explained, went only to libraries. Moreover:

> They must be required for serious research—that is to say, for an investigation calculated to advance the boundaries of knowledge. They are not lent for the purpose of private study or self-cultivation. The need, in other words, must be a matter of public concern. But with these conditions fulfilled, the library does lend. There is, of course, some risk of loss in transit, and there is also the wear and tear upon the books. There is a possibility that some book lent may be lost to posterity seeking it at Washington. There is a risk, to the charge of which I know of but one answer: that a book used is, after all, fulfilling a higher mission than a book which is merely being preserved for possible future use.[18]

"Aid to investigators" outside Washington was at the heart of Putnam's concept of rendering service to the country as a whole. The Library started publishing descriptions of its own resources in 1901 with the 1,137-page *List of Maps of America in the Library of Congress*, by Philip Lee Phillips, head of the Map Division. In the same year, it published *A Calendar of Washington Manuscripts in the Library of Congress*, compiled under the direction of manuscripts chief Herbert Friedenwald. In 1904 it began publishing important historical texts from its collections, such as the *Journals of the Continental Congress*. Putnam felt the publication of such manuscripts was "not perhaps so much a service from us as a library as a duty from us as the custodians of original sources for American history." By 1905 the Library had published bibliographies on subjects of current interest such as pensions, the Philippine Islands, and Chinese immigration. Thousands of reference inquiries were also being received and answered through the mail each year, with special attention paid to appeals for bibliographic information.[19]

Another reason for Putnam's early success was his recognition of the need for specialization, or what he called "differentiating." In "assisting forward the work of scholarship," as he testified in the 1896 hearings, the Library of Congress should also take into account "what other libraries have and are seeking to do."[20] Surveying the national scene in 1905, he pointed out that throughout the United States there was "immense activity in advanced research." Moreover, "every university is a center of such research; in a less systematic way, every community, for in this country the zest for investigation is not merely academic." He felt that public, state, academic, and privately endowed libraries each had a role to play in supporting research. In particular, there were four unique functions that the Library of Congress, as a national library, should perform for research and scholarship. It should be

1) a library for special service to the federal government; 2) a library of record for the United States; 3) a library of research which reinforces and supplements other research libraries; and 4) a library for national service, a library which shall respond to a demand from any part of the country, and thus equalize opportunities for research now very unequally distributed.[21]

To make the Library of Congress a true research library, Putnam was determined to hire scholars and subject specialists to head departments such as manuscripts, music, maps, fine arts, and law. His ability to attract distinguished scholars was crucial to the transformation of the Library of Congress into a scholarly institution. At the end of his career, discussing his relations with these scholar-specialists, Putnam gives us a clue to his success. He admitted that he could not always understand what the scholars were talking about, but he "never denied the conviction of each that his specialty was the most essential to our growth and service; my concern being merely to coordinate it with the rest, so that the elements might be fused into an organic whole."[22]

The development of the Library's collections into a nationally useful resource was constantly on Putnam's mind. To aid historical research, he felt that the national library "should be able to offer original sources." Material pertinent to a certain region "should be left to the local library having a particular duty to that locality," but "material relating to the country as a whole, to the origins, history, and operations of the Federal Government, should be left to the Library of the nation."[23] In 1903 Putnam persuaded his friend and supporter, President Theodore Roosevelt, to issue an executive order that transferred the papers of most of the nation's founders from the State Department archives to the Manuscripts Division of the Library of Congress—the beginning of the Library's presidential papers collection, which today includes the papers of the first twenty-three Presidents.

The Librarian felt that when original manuscript materials could not be acquired, facsimiles or transcripts would "render the most useful service." In 1905 he began a copying program for manuscripts relating to

American history located in foreign archives, and by 1927 over 300,000 manuscript, typewritten, or photostat copies had been added to the Library's collections. In 1925, James B. Wilbur established an endowment to support this effort, and in 1927 John D. Rockefeller made a $450,000 grant to the Library for a five-year extension of the project. This soon led to a large-scale microfilming effort under the supervision of historian Samuel Bemis. Documents were filmed in the Netherlands, Italy, Spain, Canada, and England, where one camera was set up in the House of Lords itself.[24]

There were limits, however, and by 1907 Putnam had decided it would be impractical for the Library of Congress to collect or retain governmental archives or official records. As a result, he became an early advocate of the creation of a government hall of records or national archive, and his continued support for the concept helped the National Archives come into existence in 1934.[25]

The Librarian was especially far-sighted in acquiring research materials about other countries and cultures. In 1901 he told a group of scholars that the national library "had a duty" to gather and make available to American investigators the records and imprints of other countries in the Western Hemisphere.[26] In 1904 he purchased a 4,000-volume library of Indica, owned by a professor of Sanskrit at the University of Berlin, explaining in the Library's annual report that he "could not ignore the opportunity to acquire a unique collection which scholarship thought worthy of prolonged, scientific, and enthusiastic research, even though the immediate use of such a collection may prove meager." In 1906 he boldly acquired the 80,000-volume private library of Russian literature owned by G. V. Yudin of Siberia, even sending a Library of Congress staff member to Russia to supervise the packing and shipping of the books. A 10,000-volume private collection of Hebraica was donated in 1912. Collections of Chinese and Japanese books were also acquired, and the Librarian took great pride in the establishment, in 1928, of a division of Chinese literature, which he planned to make into "the center on this hemisphere for the pursuit of oriental studies."[27]

Putnam dealt carefully with Congress, stating the Library's needs and expectations in a forthright manner. Congressmen trusted him, and the results were impressive. In 1904 the annual appropriation for books for the collection reached $98,000. By 1924 the book collection had surpassed 3 million volumes, the manuscript and music collections each contained over a million items and, thanks largely to the copyright law, the map and print collections were growing rapidly. The Library's potential services were diverse and far-reaching, but Putnam had come to the conclusion that the government had "reached about the limit in the *forms* of outlay feasible from the public treasury"; funds from other sources were needed for special functions and innovative services.[28] And, in the fall of 1924, the Librarian had an unusual proposal in hand—one he wanted to accept.

A private citizen, Elizabeth Sprague Coolidge, offered an endowment to the Library for promoting the appreciation and understanding of music. She also wanted to pay for a concert hall within the Library's building, to support the commissioning of new works of music, and to provide the chief of the Music Division with a generous honorarium. Putnam always had felt that government salaries were too low to attract and keep the distinguished scholars he hoped to head his scholarly divisions, and the Coolidge gift would mean that the chief of his Music Division would be "an expert of the requisite competence." And the expansion of activities based on the collections of the Music Division appealed to him as a way the Library, through the generosity of private citizens, could "do for American scholarship and cultivation what is not likely to be done by other agencies."[29]

Mrs. Coolidge's proposal led directly, in 1925, to the creation of the Library of Congress Trust Fund Board. It was the beginning of a new era for Putnam and the Library. A quasi-corporation established to serve as a trustee of endowments from the Library, the Trust Fund Board was chaired by the Secretary of the Treasury and had as its members the chairman of the Joint Committee on the Library, the Librarian of Congress, and two private citizens. The act establishing the board also recognized the authority of the Librarian to accept gifts and bequests in the name of the United States.

Prominent individuals such as James B. Wilbur, Archer Huntington, John D. Rockefeller, Gertrude Clarke Whittall, and many others soon joined Mrs. Coolidge as Library of Congress benefactors. Putnam was taking advantage of a new supportive relationship between private citizens and institutional collecting that developed in the 1920s, which was truly America's decade of the privately endowed, specialized research library. Between 1919 and 1932 the Huntington, Clements, Morgan, Clark, and Folger Shakespeare libraries were established by wealthy, public-spirited book collectors. As a government official, Putnam was able to make a unique national, patriotic appeal to potential donors. The success of his Trust Fund Board was of crucial importance to his vision of the nationalization of the Library's collections and services.

The Librarian felt that the effect of the private funding was to "raise the sense of government responsibility" for the growth of the Library's basic services and for its physical plant. And indeed, Congress responded generously: in the late 1920s, it increased the book budget, providing money for a new book stack and for extending existing stack levels. Moreover, in 1930, Congress spent $1.5 million to purchase the Vollbehr collection of incunabula, which included one of three perfect vellum copies of the Gutenberg Bible. The initiative for this acquisition came not from Putnam, who thought that its purchase by private funds would be more appropriate than by using government funds, but from members of

Congress and the general public.[30] Putnam felt his real victory came in 1931, when Congress authorized the construction of a new annex building. If possible, he always remained in the background, pointing first to this example of new private interest in the Library and then to that example of renewed congressional interest. But of course it was the Librarian of Congress himself who planned, executed, and then orchestrated this unique cooperative partnership, one that represented a new role for the American government in the support of learning and the arts.

The new funding of the late 1920s immensely improved service to researchers within the Library. A special study room service was established in 1927 when the stack space was expanded. When the annex building was finally completed and opened in 1938, the number of private study rooms available to "serious investigators" reached not less than 226: 52 in the main building and 174 in the annex. Book service was provided to each of these study rooms, and the scholars assigned to each also were "freely admitted to the stacks."[31]

Private endowments enabled the Librarian to establish a system of "chairs" whereby, as in the case of the chief of the Music Division, the salary of the chief of a division was supplemented. Putnam no longer had to tell Congress that he preferred not to fill a chief's position until he could offer a distinguished scholar a reasonable salary. In addition to the Music Division, chairs were established in geography, fine arts, and American history. The Librarian called these positions "interpretive chairs," for the incumbent was expected to combine administrative duties with "an active aid and counsel to those pursuing research in the Library and general research within his field."[32] The augmented salary provided by the new chair in American history, for example, allowed Putnam in 1927 to appoint the well-known historian J. Franklin Jameson as chief of the Manuscripts Division.

The notion of hiring retired scholars as consultants to help provide interpretive service was developed by Putnam soon after the first chairs were established. He explained in the first issue of *Library Quarterly*, published in January 1930, why such scholarly specialists were needed. The cataloging or reference skills of the trained librarian, he explained bluntly, while of a "high order" and of fundamental importance, were the equipment of a "professional technician." The knowledge of scholars familiar with the main fields of learning would help the Library develop the collections, perfect the technical apparatus, and assist readers in the actual use of the collections. These consultants, drawn from the ranks of retired scholars, would be paid a flat stipend. Unlike the holders of the chairs, they would have no administrative duties.[33]

Basic support for the chairs and for the consultants came from endowment funds. By 1938 there were five endowed chairs: music, American history, fine arts, geography, and aeronautics. The Librarian also envisioned, but never obtained, chairs in political science, social science, economics, jurisprudence, and international relations. There were many consultant positions, but only two, in poetry and Hispanic literature, were supported by endowments. Funds for the others were supplied mostly by grants from the General Education Board and the Carnegie Corporation. Support for the Library from both private donors and the government lessened during the Depression years of the 1930s, however, and Putnam never attained his goal of a dozen endowed consultantships.[34]

Endowments strengthened bibliographic services as well. The Library's Union Catalog, a location file of books in other libraries, was greatly expanded in the 1930s, thanks to a grant from John D. Rockefeller. By the end of the decade, the catalog included the holdings of over 700 libraries in the United States and Canada, and information about nearly 5,000 special collections. By 1938 the National Union Catalog contained over 10 million cards. Also in 1938, the Rockefeller Foundation gave a grant to the Library to help establish a photoduplication service, an important aid to researchers both at the Library of Congress and outside of Washington.

By the mid-1930s, the Librarian was concentrating so hard on raising funds to support the Library's research and scholarly roles that the professional library community quite rightly felt neglected. Putnam did not make matters better when, in 1935, he quickly rejected a proposal from the ALA that the Library of Congress consider a new function: the administration of a proposed federal library bureau that would "assume responsibility for nationwide leadership in the Library movement." Putnam felt the involvement of the Library was out of the question because it "would tend to confuse and impede the service to learning that should be the primary duty of our National Library." Instead, the bureau "should be associated with one of the executive departments of government," and indeed such a bureau soon was established in the Office of Education.[35]

Putnam's emphasis on the Library's cultural and scholarly role in the 1930s, especially his preoccupation with obtaining private funding for his consultantships, meant that some of the Library's bibliographic and processing activities suffered. All Library units reported directly to Putnam, and his attention to the consultants instead of to cataloging, for example, meant that an enormous cataloging arrearage was allowed to develop. Moreover, in the mid-1930s the Librarian battled publicly with certain members of Congress who were critical of his power and independence, especially in making appointments to the Library's staff. In 1939 Putnam felt it necessary to remind the ALA and the American Council of Learned Societies (ACLS) that the Library could use their help through public endorsement of worthwhile projects, through pressure to maintain high professional standards, and by pressure for the Library to stay out of politics. The Library's future was secure, he felt, only "if the public continues to regard the Library as its national library, respects its aims as truly cultural and its service as truly scientific, is impressed by liberal support of it from the federal treasury, and has faith that its administration is completely free from politics."[36]

When Putnam retired in 1939, his major accolades came from scholarly groups such as the ACLS and the AHA. One measure of Putnam's success in making the Library of Congress "an indispensable instrument on the American continent for the promotion of learning and the increase of knowledge,"[37] as the ACLS proclaimed, was President Franklin D. Roosevelt's determination to name a nationally known scholarly man of letters as Putnam's successor. Writer and poet Archibald MacLeish was nominated, and Congress, if not the library profession, was pleased with the President's choice.

A NATIONAL VIEW OF SCHOLARSHIP AND LIBRARY COLLECTIONS

The ALA had protested Archibald MacLeish's nomination as Librarian because MacLeish was not a professional library administrator, but the new Librarian kept a shrewd eye on all his constituencies and quickly took steps to gain the support of the library community. With help from a revitalized senior staff and advice from a special committee of professional librarians, MacLeish reorganized the Library, beginning with the processing and cataloging operations. In less than five years he incorporated into the new administrative structure the achievements of Spofford and Putnam in transforming the Library of Congress into a scholarly institution. The following is a summary of the most important of these accomplishments between 1865, Ainsworth Spofford's first year in office, and 1939, when Herbert Putnam retired.

1. The cataloging, classification, and subject analysis services developed by the Library and the extension of this "bibliographic apparatus" to other libraries were significant national achievements that benefited libraries and scholarship immensely. The work of men such as J. C. M. Hanson, head of the catalogue department, chief classifier Charles Martel, and Charles H. Hastings, head of the card section, had a unifying influence on research and scholarly activity throughout America. Uniform cataloging standards, the sharing of cataloging information, the use of the Library of Congress classification system,[38] interlibrary loan, and the sharing of location information about books through the National Union Catalog and other union lists brought—indeed forced—librarians and scholars to work together. New cooperative endeavors blossomed. The AHA, for example, established a committee on library holdings that proposed, in 1939, a detailed program for "Augmenting Materials for Research in American Libraries."[39]

Such national plans for collecting in the national interest were interrupted by World War II, but as the war came to a close, efforts were enthusiastically renewed through cooperative acquisitions projects such as the Farmington Plan and the Library of Congress Mission to Europe. In the post-war years, the Library's cataloging and bibliographic apparatus, extended to other countries and languages, was the rationale and the operating base for the Public Law 480 acquisitions and cataloging program of the 1950s, and for the National Program for Acquisitions and Cataloging (NPAC) of the 1960s. Both efforts were striking examples of cooperative activity on behalf of scholarship. The purpose of NPAC, for example, was nothing less than for the Library of Congress to acquire, insofar as possible, all library materials currently published throughout the world of value to scholarship, and to provide cataloging information for these materials promptly after receipt.[40]

2. The Library of Congress contributed significantly to the promotion and professionalization of the study of American civilization. It became, in the early years of the century, a principal center for the study of American history and culture. The establishment of the Manuscript Division, to be headed by a professional historian and developed in its early years in cooperation with the AHA, was an especially significant development. Other divisions were important too, however. The Music Division, for example, became a center for collecting American music, and the establishment in 1928 of its American folk song project was an influential innovation.

3. The bibliographic publications produced by the Library's specialists from 1901 to about 1930 were themselves major contributions to scholarship, particularly in cartography, music, genealogy, and local history. In fact, the contributions of Philip Lee Phillips and Oscar Sonneck, chiefs of the Maps and Music Divisions respectively, helped shape both cartography and music as scholarly disciplines in America. The bibliographic work of the Documents Division, headed by James B. Childs, established national and international standards for government document acquisitions and bibliography.

4. The acquisition, in the first decades of this century, of extensive research collections in foreign languages and about other countries and cultures, particularly those of Russia, the Middle East, China and Japan, made the Library of Congress an international resource for scholarship. It became a world library. The existence of these important foreign language collections shaped cooperative acquisitions efforts among American research libraries in the 1940s and 1950s and helped stimulate the area studies movement of the 1960s.

5. The Library of Congress helped to inspire increased governmental support for intellectual and scholarly activity. The monumental Library building, capped by a "torch of learning" above its gold-plated dome, symbolized a national, democratic faith in education. Of greater practical importance was increasing Congressional support for the Library's activities: between 1898 and 1938, the annual appropriation for basic Library of Congress activities increased tenfold, from $300,000 to over $3 million.[41] Thanks to Librarian Putnam, Congress took pride in its investment in the Library and began to take seriously the notion that the United States government had a responsibility to support educational, cultural, and scholarly activities. Such federal support began to grow in the 1930s, was greatly stimulated by World War II, and today plays an important role in our national life.

The Library of Congress, then, between 1865 and 1939 made important contributions to American scholarship through the development of its research collections, its cataloging and bibliographic apparatus, and its interpretive services. However, Herbert Putnam's success in nationalizing these collections and services by making them available to others was a contribution of even more fundamental importance, for it encouraged a national view of scholarship and research collections and stimulated cooperative efforts among librarians, scholars, and educators. Putnam also pioneered in bringing the federal government, private foundations, generous private citizens, and American libraries together in a partnership on behalf of books and scholarship—a partnership that has grown and flourishes in the United States today.

NOTES

1. Herbert Small, comp., *Handbook of the New Library of Congress* (Boston, 1897) 8.

2. Herbert Putnam, "The National Library: Some Recent Developments," U.S. Library of Congress, *Annual Report of the Librarian of Congress for the Fiscal Year Ending June 30, 1928* (Washington, D.C.: Government Printing Office, 1928) 331; Herbert Putnam, testimony in U.S. Congress, Joint Committee on the Library, *Condition of the Library of Congress*, 54th Congress, 2nd sess., S. Rept. 1573 (Washington, D.C.: Government Printing Office, 1897) 220; Nancy L. Benco, "Archibald MacLeish: The Poet Librarian," *Quarterly Journal of the Library of Congress* 33 (July 1976): 234-36.

3. For a summary of the development of the Library of Congress between 1865 and 1939, see John Y. Cole, ed., *The Library of Congress in Perspective: A Volume Based on the Reports of the Librarian's Task Force and Advisory Groups* (New York: R. R. Bowker Co., 1978) 10-25. Unless otherwise noted, dates and statistics are from John Y. Cole, *For Congress and the Nation: A Chronological History of the Library of Congress* (Washington, D.C.: Library of Congress, 1979).

4. Ainsworth Rand Spofford, "The Government Library at Washington," *International Review* 5 (November 1878): 769. Thomas Jefferson, letter to Samuel H. Smith, September 21, 1814, Jefferson Papers, Library of Congress.

5. See Dan Lacy, "The Library of Congress: A Sesquicentennial Review: I. The Development of the Collections," *Library Quarterly* 20 (July 1950): 157-79.

6. U.S. Library of Congress, *Annual Report of the Librarian of Congress for the Year of 1875* (Washington, D.C.: Government Printing Office, 1876) 10.

7. Library of Congress, *Annual Report 1875* 6.

8. U.S. Congress, Joint Committee on the Library, *Special Report of the Librarian of Congress*, 54th Cong., 1st sess., Sen. Doc. 7 (Washington, D.C.: Government Printing Office, 1895) 14.

9. U. S. Congress, Joint Committee on the Library, *Condition of the Library of Congress*, 54th Congress, 2nd sess., S. Rept. 1573 (Washington, D.C.: Government Printing Office, 1897) 139-68, 179-203, 216-18.

10. 29 Stat. 538 (1897).

11. For Young's career and accomplishments, see John C. Broderick, "John Russell Young: The Internationalist as Librarian," *Quarterly Journal of the Library of Congress* 33 (April 1976): 117–49.

12. For Putnam's career and accomplishments, see John Y. Cole, "Herbert Putnam and the National Library," in *Milestones to the Present: Papers from Library History Seminar V*, ed. Harold Goldstein (Syracuse, NY: Gaylord Professional Publications, 1978) 109–22.

13. Harvard College Class of 1883, *Thirtieth Anniversary, 1883–1913* (Boston, 1913) 156.

14. John Y. Cole, "Cross-Currents: BL and LC in Historical Perspective," *Library Review* 32 (Winter 1983): 252–53.

15. Herbert Putnam, "What May Be Done for Libraries by the Nation," *Library Journal* 26 (August 1901): 10–11.

16. Herbert Putnam, "The Relation of the National Library to Historical Research in the United States," in *American Historical Association Annual Report for 1901* (Washington, D.C., 1902) 115.

17. Arthur E. Bestor, Jr., "The Transformation of American Scholarship, 1875–1917," in *Librarians, Scholars, and Booksellers at Mid-Century*, ed. Pierce Butler (Chicago: University of Chicago Press, 1953) 19.

18. Herbert Putnam, "The Library of Congress as the National Library," *Library Journal* 30 (September 1905): C 30.

19. Putnam, "The Library of Congress as a National Library" C 27–34.

20. U.S. Congress, Joint Committee on the Library, *Condition of the Library of Congress* 222.

21. Putnam, "The Library of Congress as the National Library" C 28.

22. Herbert Putnam, "Remarks," in *An Address to Herbert Putnam, Librarian of Congress 1899–1939, by the American Council of Learned Societies, Together with His Reply, Washington, January 27, 1939* (Washington, D.C., 1939) [7–8].

23. Putnam, "The Relation of the National Library to Historical Research" 120.

24. Francis C. Henshaw, "A Brief History of Library of Congress Micro-Reproduction Projects," in *National Microfilm Association: Proceedings of the Eighth Annual Meeting and Convention*, ed. Vernon D. Tate (Annapolis, MD: National Microfilm Association, 1959) 220.

25. Victor A. Gambos, *J. Franklin Jameson and the Birth of the National Archives, 1906–1926* (Philadelphia: University of Pennsylvania Press, 1981) 85.

26. Putnam, "The Relation of the National Library to Historical Research" 122–23.

27. U.S. Library of Congress, *Report of the Librarian of Congress for the Fiscal Year Ending June 30, 1904* (Washington, D.C.: Government Printing Office, 1904) 27–31; *Report of the Librarian of Congress for the Fiscal Year Ending June 30, 1907* 20–29; *Report of the Librarian of Congress for the Fiscal Year Ending June 30, 1928* 6–8.

28. Herbert Putnam, "The National Library: Some Recent Developments," in *Report of the Librarian of Congress for the Fiscal Year Ending June 30, 1928* (Washington, D.C.: Government Printing Office, 1928) 334.

29. *Report of the Librarian of Congress for the Fiscal Year Ending June 30, 1925* (Washington, D.C.: Government Printing Office, 1925) 5–7.

30. Elizabeth Snapp, "The Acquisition of the Vollbehr Collection of Incunabula for the Library of Congress," *Journal of Library History* 10 (April 1975): 152–61.

31. William Adams Slade, "Some Notes on the Library of Congress as a Center for Research," in *Annual Report of the Librarian of Congress for the Fiscal Year Ending June 30, 1938* (Washington, D.C.: Government Printing Office, 1939) 452.

32. Herbert Putnam, "The National Library: Some Recent Developments," *Annual Report of the Librarian of Congress for 1928* 336.

33. Herbert Putnam, "Consultants at the National Library," *Library Quarterly* 1 (January 1930): 18-21.

34. William Adams Slade, "Some Notes," *Annual Report* 453.

35. Herbert Putnam, letter to Carl Milam, executive director of the American Library Association, January 13, 1935, Library of Congress Archives.

36. Herbert Putnam, "The Future of the Library of Congress," in *The Library of Tomorrow: A Symposium*, ed. Emily Miller Danton (Chicago: American Library Association, 1939) 180-81; Putnam, "Remarks," *An Address to Herbert Putnam*.

37. Putnam, "Remarks," *An Address to Herbert Putnam*.

38. Libraries with large research collections generally preferred the Library of Congress (LC) classification system. By 1941, 212 libraries had adopted the LC classification. A 1975 survey found that 635 four-year college and university libraries (about 55 percent of the total) were using the LC system. See Jane Aiken Rosenberg, "The Library of Congress and the Professionalization of American Librarianship, 1896-1939," Ph.D. Diss., University of Michigan, 1988, 414-15. Rosenberg's valuable dissertation documents the influence of the Library's services in many different areas.

39. American Historical Association, Special Committee on Library Holdings, *A Suggested Program for Augmenting Materials for Research in American Libraries* (Washington, D.C.: American Historical Association, 1939) 23.

40. Cole, *The Library of Congress in Perspective*, 59-60.

41. William Adams Slade, "Some Notes," *Annual Report* 454.

3

Special Collections and Academic Scholarship: A Tangled Relationship

Neil Harris

The idea and the practice of organizing rare collections and purchasing archival materials of distinct interest to scholarly investigators has been tied by some directly to the growth of the academic research library and the professionalization of scholarship. Special collections can be seen as one of the many systems of management—including the card catalog and subject classification, rationalized administration, interlibrary cooperation, specially allocated budgets, charge-out procedures, and reserve collections—that have become central to the enterprise of our academic libraries. These libraries evolved practices and structures as responses to accelerated university growth. It is difficult to deny the intimate connections linking the expanded research libraries of the late nineteenth and early twentieth centuries with the professionalization of American scholarship.

However, the timing of this marriage between university library and rare books remains puzzling. For academic libraries were by no means the first institutions in this country to develop or inherit such collections. Indeed, they were late in the field, as Phyllis Dain has made clear (see chapter 1). A series of other specialized institutions, founded during the eighteenth, nineteenth, and twentieth centuries, pioneered in the acquisition of rare books. Their histories, their functions, their purposes, and their larger roles may raise some questions about assigning priorities and offering explanations.

Neil Harris's chapter was originally prepared as a commentary on William L. Joyce's "Scholars, Librarians, and Special Collections," delivered at the 1987 Library of Congress conference from which this book derives. Dr. Joyce's paper was published in a different version in *Rare Books & Manuscripts Librarianship*, Spring 1988 (vol. 3, 19–29). Professor Harris's comments are included here because they speak so well to a number of issues raised in the papers in this collection.

By the time that Harvard's Widener Library had organized its "treasure room" in 1915, squarely within the formative period of the academic rare book collection, there were literally hundreds of rare book libraries and special collections scattered across the United States, many of them of great interest to scholars, both amateur and professional. They were not, however, primarily academic libraries, designed to serve resident faculties. Their tremendous variety baffles easy description, but several basic types together constituted something like a system.

First of all, there were the private collections of great patrons, who self-consciously collected certain texts because they were beautiful, or difficult to obtain, or prestigious to own, or expensive, or even because of some idea that such collecting would benefit American scholarship. The Morgan Library, for example, was open to scholars for use well before World War I, albeit selectively, and was used by a number of them during Morgan's lifetime. There was no question about this being anything but a noncirculating, carefully monitored, highly privileged, and specialized setting. It was of benefit chiefly to scholars and connoisseurs and was a recapitulation of some of the great private libraries gathered by European noblemen, church officials, and English gentry during the previous several centuries.

Both before and after the creation of the Morgan many other private collections were organized. Henry Clay Folger's Shakespeare materials, more than 70,000 volumes, opened in their own building in the early 1930s, a library intended, as he wrote, "to help make the United States a center for literary study and progress." Henry Huntington, whose library was built on the gatherings of great collectors like Robert Hoe, Beverly Chew, Frederick R. Halsey, Grenville Kane, and others, had established the legal entity of his library by the early 1920s, and it was already being used by scholars before his death in 1927.

These institutions formed a chapter in the lengthy and complex history of personal collecting, an extension of an older tradition of amateur scholarship in which great patrons and wealthy aristocrats invited specialists into their homes and enjoyed the reflected glory of erudite explorations. This model obviously benefited from, and benefited in turn, the process of professionalizing scholarship, but it was something different from it as well, older, and expressive of other values.

A second kind of American special library was the public private collection. This was an endowment of funds, a group of books, or both, concerned primarily, once again, with high scholarship and connoisseurship. Unlike the private libraries these collections were, in many cases, expected to have large public importance, and often reflected local pride and a sense of municipal competition. One thinks of the noncirculating collections created in Chicago's Newberry, for example, starting in the 1880s, or the assemblage of the Astor and Lenox Libraries with the Tilden Trust to constitute the research collection of the New York Public Library. The Library of Congress opened its Rare Book Division in 1927, but it was clearly engaged in the act of special collecting for scholars long before then. All this occurred at a time when university libraries were doing almost nothing with the concept of the rare book or special collections.

A third version of the specialized research library already in operation was the public archival collection, established from its beginnings partly as a record keeping operation, in part as an exercise in filio-pietism, in part as a stimulus to historical and literary scholarship. By the beginning of the twentieth century, dozens of states and cities proudly boasted their own historical societies, many of them immensely rich in local original sources—manuscripts, newspapers, local imprints, governmental records, directories, maps, photographs, and engravings—in addition to all sorts of memorabilia and antique objects, such as costumes, furniture, paintings, and commercial art.

These institutions, which would in many cases develop into combined library-museums, like those of the Chicago or New-York historical societies, and would in other cases specialize in one side of the fence or the other, were already crucial to the development of American scholarship. They were heavily exploited by the new generation of professional scholars in the early twentieth century. But they had begun to establish their special collections even in the eighteenth century—at the American Philosophical Society, for example, or the American Academy of Arts and Sciences in Boston.

There were, in fact, some 159 special libraries founded before 1850, and several hundred more during the next forty years. The collections of the New-York Historical Society included, by 1914, 5,000 volumes of newspapers, thousands of manuscript materials, and 250,000 books. The State Historical Society of Wisconsin, led first by Lyman Draper and then by Reuben Thwaites, had an even larger library of 300,000 volumes by this date, and an extraordinary set of special collections, particularly in the area of labor relations.

The state historical societies were places where scholars like Frederick Jackson Turner, George Bancroft, Francis Parkman, Moses Coit Tyler, and other did their work, decades before university libraries got into the business of special collections. And in some of these institutions, as in the New-York Historical Society's Landauer Collection, the materials being housed and cataloged were far from traditional—among them badges, buttons, paperweights, menus, wine labels, sheet music, valentines, posters, timetables, packages, and wrapping paper.

Finally, one must add the special corporate collections gathered by interest groups, religious bodies, professions, and hobbyists. These collections were meant to document the history and character of the group's activities and to encourage serious, if sometimes self-interested, research. Again, one can go back to the eighteenth century, and the libraries established by certain trades and guilds. There were church libraries and archives, with a long history of supporting scholarship, and legal and medical libraries, where scholarship and practice had somewhat different relationships than they did in academic life. All of these research libraries were functioning as types long before World War I, and were being exploited by investigators, both professional and amateur.

This truncated and barely adequate survey is relevant to our discussion because these other genres represent a somewhat different legacy of intentions and aspirations than do academic rare book collections as a whole. It may well be argued, as William Joyce has done in his working paper, "Scholars, Librarians, and Special Collections," that the academic professionalization of scholarship provided the "idea of rare books" with "its true origins. Through peer review and criticism, professional expertise extended knowledge in a variety of disciplines. This extension of knowledge accelerated the process of identifying a scholarly canon of significant texts in a number of disciplines."[1] I suggest, however, that it seems unwise to identify the creation of academic rare book collections with expanding scholarship, and, more particularly, with the scholarly canon.

American scholarship had already professionalized and expanded by the 1920s and 1930s, when there were still only a few rare book and special collections in university libraries. Scholars were visiting specialized libraries outside the universities for research projects, while satisfying other needs within the academic library itself. In the late nineteenth century, many librarians believed that specialized nonacademic libraries were the route to take. "By the prompt and liberal endowment of scores of such libraries," Alexander Nelson of the Astor Library declared in 1887 at an American Library Association meeting—in the settings already being provided by historical and scientific societies and by professional schools—the requirements of specialists could be met. Special collections was a term already in use by 1900; it referred to independent endowed collections like Crerar and Newberry, or to subject collections at libraries like the Boston Public Library. University libraries were responding to the new scholarly pressures, but not by setting up rare book collections. Indeed, there is some question as to whether rare book collections would have been the best early response to make. Let me draw on my own research patterns to indicate why.

As a historian, most of my canonical texts, if the term has any meaning in my discipline, are monographs. For many of my colleagues in English, or classics, or philosophy, these are authoritative, or variant, editions of specific works. These are found, usually, in the regular stacks of the research library. Most of my work—and I use literary sources constantly—is done outside of special collections. It requires the support of a sympathetic and well-heeled bibliographer, willing to order the new books, the missing books, the serials, and the foreign monographs on which continuing scholarship depends. On a daily basis I do not employ texts that fall within the rare books or special collections category, although I am frequently at the interlibrary loan office, asking for books that may indeed be rare but are in some other library's stacks. This, I assume, was also the practice in the era before the 1930s, when few universities had well-established rare book or special collections departments.

All scholars require, some more than others, original sources that either antedate the printing revolution or, because of their rarity or uniqueness in manuscript or printed form, must be examined in something other than microform editions. Because of their value, their fragility, their age, or their scarcity, these materials have special conditions attached to their use. They normally do not circulate, they are housed in environments that are more secure and less accessible than other parts of the library building, they can be read only at certain times and under specific supervision. They are indeed fundamental parts of humanistic research. But, as I understand the term, these are not the canons of our teaching or our scholarship. Indeed, rare books and special collections seem anything but canons. They serve as the frequently changing, highly various, personally defined, and indispensable sources of individual investigation. But their status is as powerfully a function of their costliness, as it is of their scholarly utility. Their segregation into special collections has been, on the whole, a recognition of their rarity, uniqueness, or economic value, a somewhat different basis of contiguity than offered by the classification system of the rest of the library.

If one acknowledges, then, that rare book libraries were serving scholars all over the country by the 1920s and 1930s, while university libraries were, at that point, just beginning to organize their own book collections and special collections departments, we are entitled to search for the causes of this development elsewhere than in the professionalization or expansion of scholarship. The universities came to the field late. One might ask why they came late, or indeed why they came at all.

I do not know the answer to either of these questions. But let me suggest some related areas for further investigation. They may help to make sense of this history. The first need is to examine linkages. Did other research libraries provide models that academic libraries were able to draw upon; did they set examples that academic libraries enviously admired; did they provide personnel, experiences, rivalries, or procedures that university librarians exploited? How much did they figure in discussions about setting up rare book or special collections? How explicitly was the debt recognized? And what problems were developing that made the dispersed specialized libraries and archives inadequate or inappropriate to the needs of American scholars?

This opens up a second range of questions. Why did universities decide to expend time and money on these special collections? What internal political negotiations accompanied such creations? Were positions created for faculty within libraries, were faculty demands responded to, or was it merely a growth of specialized functions within larger university libraries themselves? There is an internal administrative history that must be attended to, and without it the story of academic rare book collecting is too abstract.

There is, finally, one other element in the university's involvement with rare books that should be examined, and that concerns its larger interests in philanthropy. Collectors of rare books and manuscripts tend to be wealthy. Not all of them became as interested as Huntington or Morgan in creating their own libraries as monuments. Universities have often been grateful recipients of their generosity, and it might be excusable to treat university interest in rare book donations as part of a larger development concern. Names like Beinecke and Houghton suggest more than simply an interest in responding to professional scholarly needs. "When the history of rare book programs in universities is fully explored," Cecil Byrd wrote some thirty years ago, "it likely will be revealed that the collector was the greatest single factor in urging, or even forcing, rare book facilities on libraries." What he terms "emulousness"—once Houghton and John Carter Brown and Clements and Clark were there, Beinecke and Lilly were sure to follow—has been an organic element in university growth and library expansion.[2]

Thus any concern with the history of academic special collections would have to focus on, among other things, the relationships joining these libraries with other research institutions, their internal administrative history, the professionalization of university development, and the changing character of institutional ambition and patronage, in order to explain their timing, character, and housing.

If I deemphasize the connection between the evolution of rare book departments and high scholarship, it is certainly not to deny that these departments have been fundamental to humanistic research and have proved immensely stimulating and beneficial. It is rather to suggest that much of their value, and even more of their current appeal within university libraries, stems from the very fact that their origins lie outside the world of modern professional scholarship. Rare book departments are tightly connected to traditions of specialized collecting and amateur enthusiasm: idiosyncratic, often obsessional in character, monuments to passionate desire rather than dispassionate investigation. It is from here that they take their point of departure, rather than either the routinized world of scholarly production or the rationalized realm of data processing that characterizes the efficiently functioning library of today.

Indeed, rare book and special collections departments might be labelled as evocative atavisms within their larger institutions, bastion throwbacks to an earlier day. Like some museum collections, many rare book departments can be seen as professionally counter-cultural as well as socializing; they resist institutional incorporation while promulgating and codifying private enthusiasms. Many special collections reflect a medley of highly individual and sometimes questionable motives, among them obsessional greed, aesthetic passion, public spirit, institutional loyalty, amateur curiosity, regional patriotism, partisan politics, eccentric beliefs, elegant connoisseurship, and ethnic or racial identity. These motives, and the life histories of the collectors, are responsible for much of the color and idiosyncracy of our university libraries, which, save for size, might otherwise be practically indistinguishable from one another. And, often by serendipitous encounters, they provide happy hunting grounds for resident scholars.

But they are, as I have suggested, atavistic in a number of respects. As throwbacks they are fussier, less accessible, more resistant to rationalization than other parts of the academic library. They are costly to operate, seemingly inefficient and unpredictable; they present special preservation, storage, and cataloging problems. They can serve as cluster points for faculty and staff who are not always in sympathy with the main policies of the larger library. And these collections can radiate a sense of privilege. In many places they constitute the expressive aspect of the library building; their furnishings, their lighting, their shelved and sometimes panelled rooms, make them libraries within libraries, often more luxurious, more comfortable, more appealing physically than any other portion of the institution.

It may be possible to argue that this legacy of privilege helped extend, some decades ago, the growing distance that has apparently developed between faculty and librarians. I cannot speak to these trends. But it seems to me that the rare book or special collections departments are not the main site for this alienation. While research fashions change, the vast bulk of historical investigation and graduate training continues to focus on primary source materials. Quantitative methods and material culture studies, prosopography and epistemological self-consciousness may redefine the nature of these sources and reduce the stream of traditional rare book clients on the faculty. But not, I believe, in any fundamental way. For changing needs recover as much as they discard. If the manuscript or rare book loses some of its privileged status as a source of information, it gains it back as both an artifact and a revelation of power. Our new fascination with the history of classification, with taxonomic strategies, and with hegemonic values does not force us to abandon these materials. Rather it invests them with a newly charged set of functions. The collection itself is now part of our questioning; its history, focus, and appeal form an overlay to the functions it has traditionally performed.

More than that, special collections seems an area where librarians and faculty have remained in close affiliation. The smaller scale, personalized character, and valorization of the text one finds in these departments may be responsible for this. In what are sometimes anomic and colorless institutional settings, this part of the academic library retains some of the older, less mediated excitement, the love for books as objects as well as texts that originally inspired the successful efforts to store and display them. Rare book rooms are time capsules and museums as well as collections of records. Today's scholars are questioning the meaning of professionalization as a historical process, extending its cultural expression, and debating its consequences. They may find these collections, paradoxically enough, experimental regions: places to test arguments, make discoveries, hold classes, and generally reexamine the meaning of knowledge as personal and social experience and as statements of power and domination. It is precisely as a source of subversion that special collections may find their most powerful reasons for being, as a counter-cultural sphere within the smoothly organized world of the larger academic library.

NOTES

1. Paper prepared for conference, "Libraries and Scholarly Communication in the United States: The Historical Dimension," Library of Congress, 31 Oct. 1987, 8.
2. Cecil K. Byrd, "Rare Books in University Libraries," *Library Trends* 5 (April 1957): 441-42.

4

Research Libraries, the Ideology of Reading, and Scholarly Communication, 1876–1900

Wayne A. Wiegand

Post–Civil War America experienced significant changes, not least of which was the transformation of higher education from a rigid system emphasizing the classic languages and literature to an elective undergraduate system and the beginnings of graduate education and professional schools. Most scholars agree that the modern American university dates from this period. Its goal—to search for, identify, and communicate new knowledge—naturally influenced the development of research libraries, many of which are now numbered among the nation's best.

This paper will argue that the role the research library assumed in the scholarly communication system fostered by the modern American university in the last quarter of the nineteenth century in large part determined the way the research library profession defined its responsibilities to the research community. Perhaps a discussion of this period can shed some light on contemporary problems with which the profession struggles today. Much of what is discussed here is derived from recent reading in the history of higher education in general, and reading on what David Ricci calls "the academic culture" in particular.[1]

An understanding of the role the research library assumed in scholarly communication around the turn of the century must begin with a discussion of the ideology of reading that drove the library profession at that time.[2] Identifying the belief system about reading that governed the professional practice librarians structured for themselves during the last quarter of the nineteenth century is not difficult. Evidence for it can be found in reflections on books and reading by selected intellectuals, in self-help manuals designed to improve character, and in statements by librarians quoting the intellectuals and echoing the manuals.[3] Essentially the ideology consisted of two elements: how to read and what to read. How to read had several constituent parts. "Read with a purpose" was the first. "The best rule of reading will be a method from Nature, and not a mechanical one of hours and pages," Ralph Waldo Emerson wrote in his well-known essay on books. "Let him read what is proper to him," he continued, "and not waste his memory on a crowd of mediocrities." In *Advice to Young Men in their Conduct in Life* (1860), T. S. Arthur warned: "Mere reading . . . does not give a man much power. . . . It is *study* that does this." Frederick Harrison wrote in his *Choice of Books and Other Literary Pieces* (1886) that "reading for mere reading's sake . . . is one of the worst and commonest and most unwholesome habits we have." Ainsworth Rand Spofford, Librarian of Congress during this period, echoed these sentiments. "Have a purpose [in reading], and adhere to it with good-humored pertinacity," he admonished a class in Melvil Dewey's first library school at Columbia in 1887.[4]

"Read systematically and widely" represented the second constituent part of how to read. "Reading maketh a full man," said Sir Francis Bacon in a passage librarians loved to quote often. Emerson surmised that the opinions of Plato, Shakespeare, Milton, and Goethe, among others, carried weight with subsequent generations precisely "because they had means of knowing the opposite opinion." Identify a "course of reading," said Raymond C. Davis, director of the University of Michigan library, to Dewey's students in 1887. "It [will give you] a bird's eye view of lit[erature], and a faulty view is better than none." Spofford summarized all this neatly when he wrote in 1900: "To pursue one subject through many authorities is the true way to arrive at comprehensive knowledge."[5]

"Digest what you read" formed a third part of instructions on how to read. Authors on the subject of reading often used eating as a metaphor to describe the way the mind worked. "Some books are to be tested, others to be swallowed, and some few to be chewed and digested," said Bacon. Excessive reading, like overeating, ought to be avoided. Librarians, with many others, believed that readers ought not to introduce a new subject into their minds before digesting the one previously occupying its attention. And like the stomach, the mind had limits. "There is in many minds . . . a point of saturation," warned William Mathews in an 1876 essay, "which, if one passes by putting in more than his mind can hold, he only drives out something already in."[6]

Knowing how to read took practice. Knowing what to read was simpler. Advice abounded. Much of it was reflected in the classical curriculum, which tradition had identified as containing the appropriate cultural, intellectual, and literary norms against which new works ought to be judged. It was a curriculum many late nineteenth-century library leaders had weathered themselves, so they took to it naturally. Books and speeches were filled with lists of recommended reading. Authors cited regularly included Plutarch, Shakespeare, Homer, Dante, Milton, Burns, Tennyson, Scott, Thackeray, Dickens, and Hawthorne. In *A Book for All Readers* (1900), Spofford echoed the thoughts of others by citing history, travel, and biography as much more important than fiction. He named essay writers like Montaigne, Bacon, Newman, Emerson, and Holmes, and argued that poetry, which "deals with the highest thoughts in the most expressive language," ought to be read over and over. His list of standard selections, he pointed out, was "designed to include only the most improving and well-executed works."[7]

Improving was a word often used by individuals writing on the subject of reading. Many believed with William Foster, of the Providence Athenaeum, that the undisciplined mind was vulnerable to a "great mass of indifferent, unimportant reading," which wastes the "limited time we have in which to read," and also has a tendency toward "positively vicious and injurious books." Disciplined minds, on the other hand, discriminated between good and bad books, and with repeated practice and sound advice made the most of their reading time. To improve one's reading, Emerson posed three rules: "1. Never read any book that is not a year old. 2. Never read any but famed books. 3. Never read any but what you like." Cast in terms of today's scholarship on the creation and perpetuation of cultural, intellectual, and literary canons, Emerson was warning readers to avoid new works that had not stood the test of time, that had not met the norms forged by centuries of tradition.[8]

How to read; what to read. The structure of an ideology of reading was clear, and the vast majority of librarians came to accept it almost without question. But like all ideologies, its shortcomings were invisible to its believers. This ideology failed to acknowledge that the mental baggage readers brought to a text significantly influenced the message they got from it.[9] But that part of the ideology was missing in the public library movement of the late nineteenth century, when librarians had to deal with masses of people they believed knew neither how to read nor what to read, and when they were convinced that bad reading (as they defined it) led to bad social behavior. Attempts to implement programs motivated by the ideology are easy to trace in public librarianship. In the research library movement, however, which grew out of the changes occurring in higher education in the last quarter of the nineteenth century, the impact of the ideology is much less evident. Nonetheless, it was equally powerful in influencing the way research libraries defined their responsibilities to research communities. To understand how, one must first look closely at changes taking place in higher education at this time.

Before 1876, almost all colleges offered a classical curriculum of preselected courses that students had to take. Faculty normally required students to recite and memorize important passages from a class text, or to translate important passages from texts written in their original languages. Thus, faculty determined what students read, and how they read it. The ideology of reading was certainly in operation on the antebellum American campus, but the reading activities reflecting the ideology were put into practice by the faculty, not by academic librarians.

College librarians seldom contested this authority. Instead, they directed their attention toward developing a library practice to mime instructional methodology. For example, because institutions and their instructors did not regard independent reading very highly, college librarians felt little pressure to build large collections. Instead, they merely guarded collections donated from estates of deceased faculty members or alumni. College libraries were open for only a few hours a few days per week, and borrowing privileges for students were heavily restricted, which only further demonstrates the power of the curriculum and its agents on the antebellum college library.[10]

Two important events occurred, however, that dramatically changed higher education. The first was the publication of Charles Darwin's *Origin of Species* in 1859. Darwin's work challenged scores of established theological certainties—many of which, of course, had been echoed in the classical curriculum—and posited the tenets of a scientific method of inquiry, calling for efforts to collect facts and study them without prejudice. The second event was passage of the Morrill Act in 1862, which determined that public lands be set aside in each state to subsidize, "at least one college where the leading object shall be, without excluding other scientific and classical studies, . . . to teach such branches of learning as are related to agriculture and the mechanic arts, . . . in order to promote the liberal and practical education of the industrial classes in the several pursuits and professions in life." Colleges like the universities of Illinois and California began as a result of this act. Along with several others, like the University of Wisconsin, which "inherited" land grant status, they were strengthened by a second Morrill Act of 1890.

The land grant colleges anointed by these federal mandates grew quickly, and in time became inextricably linked with the scientific method of inquiry scholars found so convincing. Together the institution and the adoption of the scientific method created a new environment, an "academic culture." That culture consisted of experts whose job it was to find new truths to replace the old authority patterns Darwin had so successfully contested. Above all, the experts had to meet the new challenges to the social order posed by a rush of new technologies, by industrialization, by immigration and by urbanization. The universities and faculties that evolved from this mix of forces had a different goal than their antebellum predecessors. They were charged to search for, identify, and communicate new knowledge. And that new knowledge had to be based on facts, not assumptions. Naturally, the best place to gather and contemplate these facts was within the walls of a university, where experts trained in the use of the scientific method could observe, digest, and measure their value.[11]

In history, for example, the quest for fact-gathering became a passion driven by the assumption that it was a "condition for a general advance of the discipline." Demands for more data led to the acquisition of major research collections. Spofford himself noticed how the demand for Americana "has noticeably enhanced the prices of all desirable and rare books." In 1867, he had scored a significant victory in this area by acquiring the Peter Force collection for the Library of Congress. In the late nineteenth century, people like Lyman Draper and Reuben Gold Thwaites spent countless hours chasing down and acquiring collections of "facts" that members of the newly emerging professional academic discipline of history found necessary to practicing their craft.[12] Research libraries, mostly outside academe at that time, were in the vanguard of this quest.

Academics themselves also came to believe that amassing knowledge based upon analysis of facts somehow had intrinsic social value. For example, members of new social science disciplines like psychology, sociology, and political science advertised their work as a scientific form of social analysis. They suggested in the process that further study would surely uncover those elusive "truths" society needed to reestablish the certainties overturned by Darwin and to meet the problems of the Gilded Age. The truths, it was assumed, would eventually turn into a kind of knowledge that would improve both societies and individuals. One Johns Hopkins University professor recalled that his president, Daniel Coit Gilman, believed the university should offer its scholars "the unique experience of having contributed some tiny brick, however small, to the Temple of Science, the construction of which is the sublimest achievement of man."[13]

To make the task of constructing the Temple of Science manageable, the faculty began to redirect its efforts into areas of specialization. Members of the academic culture formed a series of networks, or scientific communities, reaching from coast to coast. These networks found powerful voices in the many professional associations established during these years, whose primary purpose was to define common standards of professional conduct. Among them were the American Historical Association (1884); the American Economic Association (1885); the American Statistical Association (1888); the American Mathematical Society (1888); the Geological Society of America (1888); the American Anthropological Society (1902); and the American Sociological Society (1905).

If the new university was a Temple of Science, and its academic employees the high priests of a new knowledge, the process still required a pulpit from which to disseminate these newfound truths to other members of the order. To address the needs of the academic culture, universities established and subsidized new systems of information exchange. In the new field of political science, for example, the Johns Hopkins University founded *The Johns Hopkins Studies in Historical and Political Science* in 1883. Three years later Columbia set up the *Political Science Quarterly*. In 1890, the University of Pennsylvania began the *Annals of the American Academy of Political and Social Science*, and a year later Columbia followed with *Studies in History, Economics and Public Law*.

Most professional associations and learned societies also began publishing journals. Together with university-sponsored journals, they offered forums for members to communicate the results of their fact-gathering activities. Each journal served to institutionalize a branch of learning; each helped to establish common vocational languages and to enforce occupational standards. The *American Journal of Mathematics* (1878); the *American Chemical Journal* (1879); the *American Journal of Philology* (1879); the *American Journal of Psychology* (1887); the *American Geologist* (1888); the *American Historical Review* (1891); the *Journal of Political Economy* (1892); and the *American Journal of Sociology* (1894) all began publication within a fifteen-year period.

To supplement this new army of journals, many universities also offered subsidized presses to faculty members in order to provide a conduit for lengthier scholarly studies, which commercial publishers found unprofitable. Between 1890 and 1910, Johns Hopkins, Chicago, Columbia, Harvard, Yale, Princeton and the University of California all established presses.[14]

The communication system supported by the modern university also provided members of the academic culture with a means by which to measure the worth of their peers. Academic journal and press editors, usually highly respected members of the academic culture, weighed the value of manuscripts submitted for publication by "objective" scientific standards. Some journals and presses, it was assumed, had higher standards than others. Any member of the academic culture who published in a press or journal that discipline consensus had determined was superior would raise his national reputation above those who published in presses considered less worthy. Academics soon began to build their campus reputations in large part on the basis of publications, to advance their careers on the basis of publications, and to establish national and international visibility on the basis of their publications. Because the specialized knowledge generated by the disciplinary communities accumulated so rapidly, a consensus quickly emerged that only one's disciplinary peers were capable of judging the quality of work in that discipline.

While most members of the academic culture subscribed to journals within their own discipline, and while most were able to purchase books issued from university presses, campus libraries were nonetheless expected to collect books and journals for faculty and student use as a matter of normal library practice. Thus, as a result of a greatly expanded system of scholarly communication, and because research libraries had a responsibility to collect the products of the system, faculty members could generally assume that they and their students had access to "good reading" that had weathered a prepublication filtering process run by academic peers in whom they had confidence.

Consequently, as in the classical college, the authority to determine what to read was still being exercised by the faculty. However, that authority had been transferred from an individual who assigned texts on campus to a peer evaluation system, which largely took place off-campus, and from which research libraries were excluded except as consumers. Members of the academic culture continued to determine quality; members of the research library community were charged to obtain quantity, and to impose some order on that quantity.

Academics openly recognized the nature of the situation. Only after about 1875, wrote professor Oliver Farrar Emerson in 1909, was "the buying of books [in academic libraries] . . . put on a methodical basis by men who have known what was best in the particular fields." This attitude was echoed in the preceptorial system Princeton president Woodrow Wilson pushed for in the 1890s, in which "young doctors of philosophy would 'live in the dormitories and direct the reading and studies of the student,' thus restoring 'something of the primitive democracy of college life.'"[15] In the marketplace of ideas, then, the research scholar looked upon the research library either as a place that gathered the sources he chose to study and from which he determined prevailing truths, or as a reliable consumer that provided a reasonably stable market for the products of the scholarly communication system upon which he based his career. In either case, the scholar retained the most control. He chose what to study, and he and his peers determined what should be read by defining the canons of the disciplines. In response, research libraries continued to hunt for primary source collections, and universities that subsidized journals and presses recognized an obligation to adjust university library budgets to meet the increased needs generated by the accelerated scholarly communication system.

A parallel system for establishing literary canons also influenced research library development. Initially, this system functioned outside the university. Literary periodicals like the *National Review*, the *Saturday Review*, the *Athenaeum*, the *Critic*, and the *Atlantic* assumed responsibility for determining quality literature merely by process of selection. William Dean Howells, editor of the *Atlantic*, firmly believed that because of his editorial standards the best authors published in the *Atlantic* and lesser authors published elsewhere.

Naturally, the trade publishing world recognized the market value of the existence of a hierarchy that cemented literary canons into place. Richard Brodhead calls this "the establishment of a high literary zone." At Houghton Mifflin, James Fields began issuing the very successful Riverside Literature Series, which automatically selected the "best" American authors the nation had to offer. Brodhead argues persuasively that classic American literature, "as the nineteenth century knows it," was largely determined by Howells and Fields. They canonized some writers who met their standards of literariness, ignored or dismissed others, and thus had significant influence in identifying "the best reading." Thousands of numbers of the Houghton Mifflin Literature Series were purchased by libraries across the country, and references to the value of literary guidance provided by periodicals like the *Atlantic* are numerous in late nineteenth-century library literature.[16]

For a time academics took their cues from this literary establishment operating outside academe, but gradually they assumed a greater role in formalizing, certifying, and legitimating literary canons within their own institutions. In 1896, Bliss Perry was still in the minority when he published an essay advocating the study of modern fiction in colleges and universities. Institutions of higher education had an obligation, he argued, "to send into this public, to serve as leaven, men who know good work from bad, and who know why they know it." A generation later, his views had achieved consensus. The literature professor was regarded as an authority on literature, and the university a place where good literature was identified and transmitted. That the authors whom literary scholars endorsed were generally Anglo-Saxon males, drawn from the native-born New England literary establishment, gave members of the academy little pause. Academics studied their texts to discover important truths, and the scholarly communication system naturally expanded to accommodate their findings.[17] Libraries dutifully collected the results of their careful research and actively sought "important" collections to support it.

The accelerated system of scholarly communication created an expanding body of knowledge that students could expect to find in their research libraries. Curriculum served as another important element in determining research library development. Recent scholarship argues persuasively that universities showed an impressive ability to accommodate new areas of investigation in the late nineteenth century simply by adding "fields" to their curricula. As long as money could be found to fund new positions, the field coverage principle proved an easy, comfortably self-regulating way to deal with expansion. It proved relatively painless for university administrators; new and old faculty members working within the same departments did not have to debate disciplinary issues with each other, because they did not work the same fields. Consequently, the power of each faculty member to decide what to study in his specific area of expertise, and to determine which were the authoritative works his students ought to study, went virtually uncontested. Debates on prevailing truths were reserved for externally operating scientific communities. This environment led to significant faculty influence over collecting practices at research libraries.

The establishment of graduate programs gave faculty even more power over the direction of research library collections. Graduate students were expected to debate old assumptions by becoming acquainted with the latest research in the field under study; they were also expected to engage in wide reading. The seminar gave graduate students an opportunity to do some original research; it also created a need for easily accessible collections of primary source material. Naturally, graduate faculty pressed university libraries on their campuses to accelerate efforts to acquire larger collections of primary and secondary source materials for their students. And research libraries responded as best they could, some better than others.

Young Ph.D.s who had successfully negotiated graduate programs took jobs in colleges and universities throughout the country, where they sought to duplicate the intellectual excitement of their alma mater. For example, by 1886—only ten years after opening its doors—Johns Hopkins had granted doctorates to sixty-nine people, fifty-six of whom went on to teach at a total of more than thirty colleges and universities.[18] In their new posts, they undoubtedly pressed for teaching and research facilities similar to those they found in Baltimore.

The influence of an ideology of reading combined with the late nineteenth-century rise of an academic culture, significantly affected the development of research libraries. What students were assigned to read in higher education classes introduced them to a part of "the good reading" in a particular field. But to back up required reading assignments, academics could also count on whole libraries of good reading that had been approved for publication by peers in whom they had confidence. Research libraries were not a part of this process, except for the pressure they could apply as consumers.

An ideology of reading was still operating here, but to members of the academic culture, whether students or faculty, the research library was not perceived as an active participant. How to read was being evaluated by a system of grading that faculty members exercised on their graduate and undergraduate students. What to read was being determined by class assignments on campus, in judgments rendered on manuscripts submitted for publication in scholarly journals and presses, and in a reviewing process generated by off-campus authorities. Good research libraries had what students and faculty needed; poor ones did not. Faculty continued to determine the best reading, and from their perspective the research library had two major responsibilities. One was to remain part of the system of scholarly communication by supplying current periodicals and publications. The other was to garner as many collections of primary source materials as possible, so that research scholars did not have to travel great distances to conduct their research. Beyond these needs, faculty had little reason to concern themselves with the development of research librarianship.

To suggest that research libraries merely responded to the "supply on demand" nature of the scholarly communication system, however, distorts the total picture. At the center was an ideology of reading that governed the library's collection activities and allowed authority to remain largely in the hands of members of the academic culture. But by the late nineteenth century, the research library itself had evolved into a bureaucracy. It had developed systems of its own, tied to faith in a science of administration and in the development of a particular form of professional expertise. The library science that grew up in the last quarter of the nineteenth century called for a marriage of efficient institutional management with a unique expertise that imposed order on the cultural, intellectual, and literary objects libraries chose to collect and preserve.

Research libraries drew from this library science to fit their particular needs. They adopted or developed classification systems and subject bibliographies for patron use, and hired staff to maintain the systems. They also acquired and developed impressive special collections of primary sources, along with the staff necessary to maintain these collections. And it is during this period that formal reference librarianship had its origins. Research libraries performed admirably here too. They established and developed reference collections, and again hired staff to maintain them.[19] But no matter how hard they tried, no matter the quality of their library science, research libraries had difficulty countering the "supply on demand" attitude of resident faculty as the latter's most important criterion for evaluating service. As long as the supply was satisfactory for those faculty who used the library, they had little reason to include the research library in their thoughts about research, learning, literacy, and higher education.

These conclusions may seem harsh, but they should not be taken to imply that the research library lacks a significant role in the system of scholarly communication. Far from it. This essay attempts to reconstruct the developing role of research libraries in the system of scholarly communication as viewed by members of the academic culture. But that view is myopic, because it fails to account for the major contributions of research libraries to the dynamics of scholarship.

New scholarship is challenging the "Temple of Science" mentality, arguing that the scientific objectivity supposedly exercised by members of the academic culture is and has been molded by that culture's own limitations. Recent works show how the exclusion of entire groups of people from cultural, intellectual, and literary canons has had a major impact on how a pluralistic society looks at itself and at the histories of its various parts. Gerald Graff, for example, notes that even though scholars were motivated by "a genuine democratic egalitarianism," the academic literary studies that developed during the Progressive era nonetheless "combined class, ethnic and gender prejudices." David Ricci concludes from his research on the late nineteenth-century political science profession that "any idea advanced in political science literature must be judged cautiously on its merits as a product of an organizational environment rather than accepted automatically because practitioners certify it as a valuable addition to our knowledge of public affairs." Richard Brodhead is more specific. "Traditions begin when the past is purged of irrelevance," he says. "They come into existence when the full past, the sum of what has been, is allowed to fall from mind; then, when a past worth remembering is selected and given memorable shape." Elaine Showalter is even more forthright: "Feminist critics do not accept the view that the canon reflects the objective value judgments of history and posterity," she says, "but use it instead as a culture-based political construct. In practice, 'posterity' has meant groups of men with the access to publishing and reviewing that enabled them to enforce their view of 'literature' and to define a group of 'classics.'"[20]

Over the years, these critics argue, members of the academic culture have tended to study white male wielders of power. As a result, the cultural, intellectual, and literary canons they created and perpetuated, which in turn are reflected strongly in the collections of research libraries across the country, systematically (but seldom intentionally) excluded whole groups of people.

It is here that the research library assumes a vital role in the scholarly communication system. The library has the potential to check the built-in limitations of scholarly truth-seekers. Brodhead argues that "canons do not become available for a new group's remaking until they have already lost their compelling reality for a strategic position of their original supporters."[21] As a new generation dismantles the set of old canons that served its predecessors, and as that new generation constructs a new set of canons more carefully tailored to its own needs, it requires data saved from the past in order to redefine the past for itself. Often that data is found in research libraries.

Some authors, such as Emily Dickinson, and entire genres of literature, such as female-authored mid-nineteenth-century romances, have been rescued from relative obscurity because a few research libraries saw fit to collect them, even though the works had not been legitimated by members of the contemporary academic culture. Some works have now entered the existing canons. But "literary institutions work in part by *making* literary pasts," Brodhead argues. "They institute a particular formation of literature by making some segment of previous writing to be the significant past—a past that, reinternalized by the readers and writers who inhabit that institution, helps naturalize and validate its definition of what literature is."[22]

Other authors, like Mrs. E.D.E.N. Southworth, await a restructuring of the canon to take into account the historical context in which they worked before they can be studied. "For a work to become a source of tradition, a later worker must locate it as a significant model," Brodhead says. Showalter echoes these sentiments. "As the works of dozen of women writers have been rescued from what E. P. Thompson calls 'the enormous condescension of posterity,' and considered in relation to each other," she writes, "the lost continent of the female tradition has risen like Atlantis from the sea of English literature."[23] The same dynamics are evident in the cultural and intellectual canons governing the direction of all academic disciplines.

Some authors, some books, and whole groups of subcultures, however, will never be studied, not because they do not merit analysis, but because records of their existence have not been preserved. Research libraries must share some responsibility for their absence. This situation will undoubtedly be exacerbated in the future when research libraries have to make decisions about which materials deteriorating on their shelves deserve to be preserved, and which should be allowed to deteriorate. If they must fall back on the canons of their own contemporary culture to make these decisions, they will be sentencing future generations to an increasingly narrow view of the past, from which those generations will reconstruct their own version of the past.

Research libraries, bureaucracies within universities supporting academic cultures, deserve some credit for saving segments of a larger cultural, literary, and intellectual heritage than the contemporary academic culture considers worthy of study; but it is also necessary to recognize that research librarians are products of an academic culture. They need to become much more aware of their shortcomings, so that they do not systematically (and certainly not intentionally) erase the record of existence of entire groups functioning almost invisibly within contemporary society, and operating outside the confines of subjects being studied by members of the academic culture.

Librarians also need to become aware of the limits placed upon their professional vision by adhering to the traditional ideology of reading. The ideology is inherently flawed by the notion of identifying the "best reading," and it reverberates throughout the system of scholarly communication. For example, Spofford's belief that "the works most frequently reprinted in successive ages are the ones which it is safe to stand by" ignores the power of canons to control a circumscribed vision of the past.

This power justifiably merits the criticism of Graff, Brodhead, Ricci, Showalter, and Hamerow, to name only those cited in this paper. An ideology of reading that aims at collecting the best, then, may hinder more than help the scholars of the future, but like all ideologies it will be difficult to challenge.

To expect members of the academic culture to admit openly that they may not have considered all relevant "significant models," or that they failed to consider problems inherent in the "enormous condescension of posterity," would run counter to human nature. After all, professors are employed as experts; they are supposed to know the right answers. Research libraries may, in fact, serve as uncomfortable reminders that over time their supposedly scientific answers show many unscientific flaws. It represents a curious dichotomy. On the one hand, research libraries provide the evidence that the academic culture needs in order to prove its own expertise. On the other hand, research libraries also provide the evidence to hold that expertise suspect. The easy way out is to ignore this dichotomy. Little wonder members of the academic culture tend to overlook research libraries in their discussion of research, learning, literacy, and higher education.

Research libraries also play a vital role in the activities of the academic culture through the indirect pressure they exert as consumers. Too often, members of the academic culture appear blind to the educational benefits that accrue in libraries, and that the research library makes possible simply because it is the major consumer of scholarly materials. The ideas professors develop in their publications are often introduced in their classrooms, where they help stimulate learning experiences. Because research libraries constitute the primary market for the majority of their publications, they can justifiably take some credit for the creation of these learning experiences.

A final reason for believing research libraries play a vital role in the activities of the academic culture relates to the evaluation system that members of the academic culture have invented to judge each other's work. Academic cultures—like most cultures of the intellect—consist, for the most part, of people with good minds; but good minds which can be improved. Here the evaluation process for scholarly publications serves a useful purpose, because the evaluation usually leads to revisions that often significantly improve the work's ideas.[24]

The system of scholarly communication exists, like it or not. Research librarians and other members of the academic culture have to deal with it. But perhaps they tend to concentrate too much attention on its faults, and to ignore its strengths. Research librarians often lament the pressure that numbers exert on research library collections, yet forget the side benefits brought by the creation of these collections. Without research libraries to provide the market for these products, would the process be significantly inhibited? Many members of the academic culture have commented that colleagues who have not published for years after obtaining tenure often continue to espouse ideas that no longer fit the times and no longer fit the needs of the students they teach. The evaluation process that precedes publication does have beneficial effects on higher education; those effects might be threatened if research libraries had to cut so far back on budgets that most products no longer had a market.

Research libraries are generally left out of contemporary discussion of research, learning, literacy, and higher education in America because most experts in the academic culture who discuss such subjects perceive research libraries either as depositories for the primary sources they wish to study or as a final resting place in the scholarly communication process. The evaluation, the determination of what is best, has in large measure already taken place before the scholarly work has found its way into the research library. That the authorities to whom society looks for expert opinion do not have research libraries primarily in mind may explain why the library profession does not command much power compared to other professions.

In part librarianship has itself to blame. The profession has tied itself to an ideology of reading that in effect restricts its role in the canon-making process. The library is a cultural, literary, and intellectual institution that echoes the expert opinions of others by defining the parameters of collection building according to those expert opinions.

But one should not disparage this situation. Certainly it has worked to the benefit of millions over the past century. Certainly one can demonstrate that the academic culture and the system that supports it have had a major and positive impact on society. And certainly the process within academic culture leading to publication has beneficial spillover effects that ought to be accelerated and amplified.

But the situation also brings with it limitations, and research libraries need to be made much more aware of these limitations. If research libraries and their employees can augment that awareness, if they can turn some of their attention away from the administration of library bureaucracy and the expertise unique to it alone, perhaps the research library can play an even larger, more active role in the process of canon-making. This would require, however, significant shifts in an ideology of reading, including an acknowledgment that people interact with texts differently, often much differently and in many more ways than the reviewer in *Choice*, the *American Historical Review*, or the *New York Times Book Review* can envision by him or herself. "Best" is a relative term; recognizing that fact may be a first step toward assuming a lager role in the process of scholarly communication.

NOTES

1. David Ricci, *The Tragedy of Political Science: Politics, Scholarship and Democracy* (New Haven: Yale University Press, 1984). A good portrait of the closeness of this culture viewed from the inside is Merton Dillon, *Ulrich Bonnell Phillips: Historian of the Old South* (Baton Rouge: Louisiana State University Press, 1985). See also Burton Bledstein, *The Culture of Professionalism: The Middle Class and the Development of Higher Education in America* (New York: W. W. Norton, 1976).
2. I take my definition of ideology from Martin Seliger: a "belief system" that serves a group of people "on a relatively permanent basis." See Martin Seliger, *Ideology and Politics* (New York: The Free Press, 1976) 120.
3. A good bibliography of nineteenth-century self-help manuals can be found in Karen Halttunen, *Confidence Men and Painted Women: A Study of Middle-Class Culture in America, 1830-1870* (New Haven: Yale University Press, 1982) 248-55.
4. Ralph Waldo Emerson, "Books," in *Society and Solitude: Twelve Chapters* (Boston: Houghton Mifflin Co., 1912) 194; T. S. Arthur, *Advice to Young Men in Their Conduct in Life* (Philadelphia, 1860) 78; Frederick Harrison, *The Choice of Books and Other Literary Pieces* (London, 1886) 6. Spofford's lecture can be found in an unpublished manuscript: Francis Miksa, "Melvil Dewey's School of Library Economy, Columbia College, 1887-1888: Shorthand Notes of Classes," (1987): lecture 116, p. 1.
5. Francis Bacon, "Of Studies," in *The Essays or Counsels, Civil and Moral, of Francis Bacon*, ed. Samuel Harvey Reynolds (Oxford, 1890) 342; Ralph Waldo Emerson, "Culture," in *The Conduct of Life* (Boston: Houghton Mifflin, 1904) 141; Miksa, "Melvil Dewey's School of Library Economy," lecture 103, pp. 1,2; Ainsworth Rand Spofford, *A Book For All Readers: Designed as an Aid to the Collection, Use, and Preservation of Books and the Formation of Public and Private Libraries* (New York: G. P. Putnam's Sons, 1900) 284.
6. Francis Bacon, "Of Studies" 342; William Mathews, "Professorships of Books and Reading, Part II," in U.S. Bureau of Education, *Public Libraries in the United States of America: Their History, Condition, and Management, Special Report, Part I* (Washington, D.C.: Government Printing Office, 1876) 242. This report is one of the library profession's landmark publications. For a recent discussion of the eating metaphor, see Catherine Sheldrick Ross, "Metaphors of Reading," *Journal of Library History* 22 (1987): 147-63.
7. Spofford, *A Book for All Readers*, chap. 1. See also Samuel Smiles, "The Companionship of Books," in *Character* (London: John Murray, 1907) 297, 322-23; and Newell Dwight Hilles, *A Man's Value to Society: Studies in Self-Culture and Character* (Chicago, 1894) 240.
8. William E. Foster, *Libraries and Readers* (New York, 1883) 20; Emerson, "Books" 196.
9. For example, see Jane P. Tompkins, ed., *Reader-Response Criticism: From Formalism to Post-Structuralism*, (Baltimore: Johns Hopkins University Press, 1980); Susan R. Sulieman and Inge Crossman, eds., *The Reader in the Text: Essays on Audience and Interpretation* (Princeton: Princeton University Press, 1980); Judith Fetterley, *The Resisting Reader: A Feminist Approach to American Fiction* (Bloomington: Indiana University Press, 1977); Elizabeth Freund, *The Return of the Reader: Reader-Response Criticism* (London: Methuen, 1987); and especially Wolfgang Iser, *The Act of Reading: A Theory of Aesthetic Response* (Baltimore: Johns Hopkins University

Press, 1978) and Stanley Fish, *Is There a Text in This Class? The Authority of Interpretive Communities* (Cambridge, MA: Harvard University Press, 1980). See also Janice Radway, *Reading the Romance: Women, Patriarchy and Popular Literature* (Chapel Hill: University of North Carolina Press, 1984) for a recent attempt to evaluate a literature through the eyes of the regular readers of that literature.

10. Frederick Rudolph, *Curriculum: A History of the American Undergraduate Course of Study since 1636* (San Francisco: Jossey-Bass Publishers, 1977) 69. See also Gerald Graff, *Professing Literature: An Institutional History* (Chicago: University of Chicago Press, 1987) 34–35. The standard history of the classical college library is Louis Shores, *Origins of the American College Library, 1638–1800* (New York: Barnes & Noble, 1934). See also Arthur Hamlin, *The University Library in The United States* (Philadelphia: University of Pennsylvania Press, 1981), chaps. 1–3; and Orvin Lee Shifflet, *The Origins of Academic Librarianship* (Norwood, NJ: Ablex, 1981), chaps. 1–2.

11. Ricci, *Tragedy of Political Science* 33. See also Thomas S. Haskell, *The Emergence of Professional Social Science: The American Social Science Association and the Nineteenth-Century Crisis of Authority* (Urbana: University of Illinois Press, 1977) 65ff. Standard works on Darwin's impact include Richard Hofstadter, *Social Darwinism in American Thought* (Philadelphia: University of Pennsylvania Press, 1944); Cynthia Eagle Russett, *Darwin in America: The Intellectual Response, 1865–1912* (San Francisco: W. H. Freeman and Co., 1976); and Walter P. Metzger, *Academic Freedom in the Age of the University* (New York: Columbia University Press, 1955). The best overview of these developments is still Robert Wiebe, *The Search for Order, 1877–1920* (New York: Hill and Wang, 1967).

12. Theodore S. Hamerow, *Reflections on History and Historians* (Madison: University of Wisconsin Press, 1987) 48, 166–67. See also Spofford, *A Book for All Readers* 454; and Ricci, *The Tragedy of Political Science* 55, 67.

13. Edward Shils, "The Order of Learning in the United States: The Ascendency of the University," in *The Organization of Knowledge in Modern America, 1860–1920*, ed. Alexandra Oleson and John Voss (Baltimore: Johns Hopkins University Press, 1979) 28. Gilman is quoted in Ricci, *Tragedy of Political Science* 23.

14. Hamerow, *Reflections on History and Historians* 40; Ricci, *Tragedy of Political Science* 50; Graff, *Professing Literature* 62.

15. Oliver Farrar Emerson, "The American Scholar and the Modern Language," *PMLA* 24 (1909): appendix xc; John Kennedy Winkler, *Woodrow Wilson: The Man Who Lives On* (New York: Vanguard Press, 1933) 85, as quoted in Graff, *Professing Literature* 92.

16. Richard Brodhead, *The School of Hawthorne* (New York: Oxford University Press, 1986) 62, 86, 87–88, 101. Most research libraries still own numerous Riverside editions. For an example of the influence that periodicals occupying a high literary zone had on the acquisition of fiction by libraries, see discussion of a new periodical entitled *Novel-List* in *Library Journal* 12 (1887): 537. See also Spofford, *A Book for All Readers* 243–244.

17. Bliss Perry, "Fiction as a College Study," *PMLA* 11 (1896): 84. American modernism's ability to encompass a wider range of intellectual, cultural, and literary canons did not seriously threaten the authority of academic and literary experts to determine the canon. For a wide-ranging recent discussion of modernism's many influences, see *American Quarterly* 39 (1987), a special issue on

"Modernist Culture in America." See also Brodhead, *The School of Hawthorne* 60–61; and Graff, *Professing Literature* 68.

18. W. Carson Ryan, *Studies in Early Graduate Education: The Johns Hopkins University, Clark University, The University of Chicago* (New York: Carnegie Foundation, 1932) 32; Ricci, *Tragedy of Political Science* 35–36.

19. For a more extended discussion of the changing library bureaucracy at this time, see Wayne A. Wiegand, "View from the Top: The Library Administrator's Changing Perspective on Standardization Schemes and Cataloging Practices in American Libraries, 1891–1901," in *Reference Services and Technical Services: Intersections in Library Practice*, ed. Gordon and Sally Stevenson (New York: Haworth Press, 1983) 11–27.

20. Graff, *Professing Literature* 13–14, 173; Ricci, *Tragedy of Political Science* 291; Brodhead, *School of Hawthorne* 206; Elaine Showalter, ed., *The New Feminist Criticism: Essays on Women, Literature and Theory* (New York: Pantheon, 1985) 32. This literature continues to grow. See also Kermit Vanderbilt, *American Literature and the Academy: The Roots, Growth and Maturity of a Profession* (Philadelphia: University of Pennsylvania Press, 1987); Jane Tompkins, *Sensational Designs* (New York: Oxford University Press, 1985); and Gerda Lerner, *The Creation of Patriarchy* (New York: Oxford University Press, 1986).

21. Brodhead, *School of Hawthorne* 206.

22. Brodhead, *School of Hawthorne* 83.

23. Brodhead, *School of Hawthorne* 176; Showalter, *New Feminist Criticism* 27.

24. In a recent article discussing the excessive number of historical inaccuracies and shortsighted, self-serving interpretations of the Age of Discovery in popular American history textbooks, James Axtell makes this point forcefully. "Pressure the better journals into the regular reviewing of textbooks," he argues, and most of the sloppy delivery of information will disappear. See James Axtell, "Europeans, Indians and the Age of Discovery in American History Textbooks," *American Historical Review* 92 (June 1987): 632.

5

Preservation, Library Collections, and the Concept of Cultural Property

Paul N. Banks

KINDS OF VALUES: MEDIUM AND MESSAGE

Every idea, every image, every quantitative datum, is recorded in or on a physical medium: a book, a manuscript, an instrument chart, an optical digital disc, even the human brain. A fundamental characteristic of research collections in libraries, then, is that their constituent records are at once medium and message. This given is accompanied by two corollaries. First, the physical container of information, the medium, constitutes information also. Second, although the physical medium can be represented in illustrations or in two- or three-dimensional facsimiles, it can never truly be duplicated. These facts are immutable, and as such they are perhaps less interesting for themselves than for what they call to our attention. The point at which discourse must begin is the difficult question of the relative significance, usefulness, and importance of medium and message.

It is common in discussions of preservation in the library world to make an apparently straightforward distinction between "information" or "intellectual content" on the one hand, and "artifact" on the other. However, the interrelationship between medium and message is more complex than this simple dichotomy would suggest, and understanding the interrelationship is fundamental to making appropriate preservation decisions for individual records or classes of records. Before we look at the idea of cultural property, it may be useful to look at some of these complexities, especially the significance of the medium.

Records are most likely to be important for the explicit information that they contain: the text of a book or document, the image of a map, the sound of a tape recording. The explicit information per se, the intended message, can often be copied with little or no loss of meaning; that is, it can be manipulated or consulted independently of the original physical medium in which it was embodied. Reprints and today's ubiquitous photocopies and microforms have became indispensable tools of scholarship. The information that is embodied in the medium itself—the physical container of the message—presents more complex issues of consultation, dissemination, and preservation.

The relationship between medium and message is in part exemplified in G. Thomas Tanselle's discussion of the distinction necessary to analytical and descriptive bibliographers between the work—for example *Moby Dick*, which exists in myriad editions and reprints—and the book—a particular state of *Moby Dick* that may be important for bibliographical or textual studies.[1] In the latter case, it is mainly physical details that are the immediate subject of study, even where the larger end is to understand the relationship between the work and its author, its publisher, and its readers. The distinction between medium and message may be blurred, perhaps to the point of extinction, in such cases as fine press and artist's books in which (echoing Marshall McLuhan) the medium to a large extent is the message, especially if the text is a reprinting of material available elsewhere.

Much of the information that inheres in the physical medium can if necessary be described in verbal and quantitative terms (the color of a binding or dimensions of the pages), or represented visually in a copy or facsimile, with varying degrees of precision, detail, and cost. Descriptions of the physical record are used to serve a variety of ends both scholarly and managerial. Obvious and ubiquitous examples are the statements in library catalogs and bibliographic databases of dimensions, number of pages, any unusual physical features and, if other than a book, format. Such descriptions are useful for managerial and service functions. Managers will want to know, for example, if a book is small enough to fit on normal-sized shelves or must be shelved in a separate section of oversized books. Users, on the other hand, will want to know if the information is in the form of a book that can be used independently of any reading equipment, or is in a microform or database that can only be used on a viewer or terminal in a fixed location. More extensive descriptions of physical features of books and manuscripts may be found in bibliographies, exhibition catalogs, and sometimes monographs. For example, historical bibliographies may include a collation, and exhibition or collection catalogs or monographs may have extensive descriptions of paper, typefaces, illustration media, bindings, or other physical features.

The representation of a physical object in a facsimile (here used to mean a visual copy intended to convey some physical characteristics) is in some senses an intermediate step between a copy of the explicit information, as for example a transcription, and the object itself. Facsimile representations have two uses that are relevant to the present discussion. First,

THE CONCEPT OF CULTURAL PROPERTY

they provide a more detailed representation of the visual qualities of an object than a verbal description (while usually representing the message as well), and second, they also may reduce the need for direct access to important or vulnerable original objects.

The relationship of a representation of a physical object and the object itself depends in part in how faithful the facsimile is. It is now possible to produce relatively faithful two-dimensional facsimiles by photographic or photomechanical means. Three-dimensional facsimiles present serious craft and cost challenges rather than photomechanical difficulties, as the bindings of such expensive facsimiles as the Domesday Books attest. It perhaps does not need to be pointed out that the original object must exist in order to be so described or facsimiled, and it should also be kept in mind that when improvements in reproduction processes make a better facsimile possible, the original must be directly rephotographed as the source for the new facsimile.

But there are questions that go considerably beyond simple convenience or economy where the physical medium itself carries information that needs to be consulted, preserved, or transmitted. By definition, authenticity cannot be duplicated. Other characteristics, such as ultimate chemical composition, that may be important in technical studies, dating, and authentication, require use of the original. Some information, especially structural and tactile, could perhaps in theory be duplicated, but the enormous effort and cost that would be involved limit the practicability of what in any case would be a questionable enterprise. The limited number of fakes of books and manuscripts (with the exception of autographs, which are often single sheets) perhaps attests as much to the effort involved in creating a plausible fake as it does to the relatively lower value of books and manuscripts compared with antiquities and works of art.

There are, then, a number of reasons why books as physical objects may assume considerable value beyond simply being containers for what I call their explicit information. In addition to their possible value as physical documents, they may have great meaning because of people or events associated with them. Whatever the basis for the value people may attach to books, that value would seem to imply some degree of responsibility for their preservation. But responsibility by whom, and for whom?

BOOKS AND MANUSCRIPTS AS CULTURAL PROPERTY

During 1982/83 T. Cullen Davis and his pastor, the television evangelist James Robison, smashed what was claimed to be more than $1 million worth of oil millionaire Davis's oriental jade and ivory sculpture because they were "graven images."[2] Did he have a legal right to do this? A moral right?

Interest in objects of age or beauty or strong associations is hardly new. Romans collected Greek sculpture; Isidore of Seville in the seventh century spoke of people who collected books for their bindings;[3] Richard de Bury in 1345 deplored the loss of classical texts just as Petrarch was beginning the humanists' search for surviving ones, and Great Britain had an office of King's Antiquary in the sixteenth century, as did Sweden in the seventeenth.[4] But the idea that cultural property constitutes a category of objects of special significance to humankind, and that it thus requires special forms of protection, is of relatively recent origin, and has grown largely out of international law. The term cultural property does not appear as such in dictionaries and encyclopedias, and there is relatively little literature on the subject.

Some of the historical forces that have led to the development of the concept of cultural property will be discussed in this paper, along with some definitions. I will then attempt to demonstrate that research collections of library materials are part of the continuum of cultural property; that there are various national and international legal norms that are in part, at least, applicable to library collections; and finally that the literature of librarianship does not reflect awareness of the worldwide concern with cultural property.

With one important exception, cultural property consists of artifacts of tangible and authentic objects. In addition, to use the criteria of Paul Philippot, art historian and former director of the International Centre for Conservation in Rome, objects must "embody creative quality, documentary significance, or impact on human consciousness" to qualify as cultural property.[5] Recognizable categories of cultural property have emerged, largely from the body of national laws and international treaties and conventions, about which more will be said below. First, a distinction is often made between movable and immovable cultural property. In the latter category, which is of only indirect interest to us, are buildings, monuments, and historic sites and districts.

Among movable objects, works of art have the longest tradition of implied or explicit designation as cultural property, with archaeological objects following closely. The earliest pleas for protection of cultural property were for monuments and works of art, but manuscripts, books, archives, and libraries have been included explicitly, along with scientific collections, in nearly all such codifications from the time of the Lieber Code of 1863 (see below). The definition of cultural property in the 1954 Hague Convention for the Protection of Cultural Property in the Event of Armed Conflict is indicative:

For purposes of the present Convention, the term "cultural property" shall cover, irrespective of origin or ownership:

(a) movable or immovable property of great importance to the cultural heritage of every people, such as monuments of architecture, art or history, whether religious or secular; archaeological sites; groups of buildings which, as a whole, are of historical or artistic interest; works of art; manuscripts, books and other objects of artistic, historical or archaeological interest; as well as scientific collections and important collections of books or archives or of reproductions of the property defined above;

(b) buildings whose main and effective purpose is to preserve or exhibit the movable cultural property defined in sub-paragraph (a) such as museums, large libraries and depositories of archives, and refuges intended to shelter, in the event of armed conflict, the movable cultural property defined in sub-paragraph (a);

(c) centres containing a large amount of cultural property as defined in sub-paragraphs (a) and (b), to be known as "centres containing monuments."[6]

It is especially relevant to our concern with libraries that in some cases it is collections, not all components of which would qualify individually, that constitute cultural property.

Early interest in the care of documents, works of art, and monuments was often related to perpetuating religion or glorifying a ruler. Particularly insofar as records are concerned, those objects that did not serve, or especially that were perceived to disserve, the immediate purposes of those who had control of them were neglected or simply destroyed. The neglect of the Codex Sinaiticus, for example, one of the earliest extant manuscripts of the Greek Bible, and other important early manuscripts in Greek and Middle Eastern monasteries, is described by Deuel, and Bernal vividly discusses how religious prejudice led the Spanish to destroy systematically a whole range of cultural products of the indigenous civilization in Mexico.[7]

The collection and preservation of what we now call cultural property involves a number of seemingly deep-seated human impulses, including acquisitiveness, love of beauty, and a nostalgic longing for other times or places. These impulses do not in themselves, however, comprise a basis for the doctrine that some objects are important enough to mankind as a whole that a special category needs to be constructed for thinking and acting about them. One may identify several major, and relatively recent, changes in mankind's perception of itself that have had a profound influence on the development of the idea that cultural property matters.

C. V. Wedgwood speaks of the perception, which began to change only with the Renaissance, that "the individual life was set not in time, but in eternity; ideas and actions were to be thought of not in terms of time past and time future, but in terms of eternity in Heaven or Hell."[8] It is difficult for us today, when growth in the rate of change in human affairs is so great and we so take for granted the perception of our place in a continuum of past and future, to recognize that "not until the Renaissance did a sense of the historical past as a set of separate realms become habitual, even among the educated."[9] But this consciousness brought with it awareness of how fleeting human objects and institutions are, and thus the possibility of real loss of the past. It was at once an acknowledgment of the pastness of the past and of the importance to the human spirit of continuity with it. In other words, the past would no longer necessarily survive on its own accord; conscious effort must be applied to ensure continuity.

The historian Michael Hunter, writing on the "Preconditions of Preservation," describes the change since the Renaissance from a vague respect of the past, which has existed since time immemorial, to a more critical view of older times. "This is the sense of 'history' of which modern scholarship is the heir, characterized by a preoccupation with historical change, an acute sense of anachronism, and a stress on the importance of the accurate study of past periods, often undermining their sentimental appeal."[10] Another trend of the Renaissance—indeed, one that in part defines it—was elevation of the status of artists and works of art. The artist had before been considered essentially an artisan, who might be hired to serve the relatively utilitarian purpose of decorating an altar or creating a didactic picture. Then, under the influence of such figures as Leonardo da Vinci and Giorgio Vasari, and through the patronage of the great Renaissance collectors, a work of art came to be seen as an act of creation, a unique manifestation of the human spirit.[11]

Progress toward societal protection of cultural property was set back, however, by the intolerance unleashed by the Protestant Reformation and the Catholic Counter-Reformation. There are many familiar examples in the realm of the arts, such as the dispersal of Van Eyck's Ghent altarpiece, and the defacing of statuary on Gothic churches and cathedrals in France and the Netherlands. More relevant to our concern is the way both Protestants and Catholics burned each other's written works. One can only wonder, for example, how many manuscripts were damaged or destroyed as a result of the dissolution of the monasteries in Great Britain under Henry VIII.

During the Enlightenment, educated people became passionately interested in describing, studying, categorizing, and cataloging objects and phenomena; in other words, they attempted to order the universe as a means of trying to understand it. The rationalism and progressivism of this era, of which many aspects were translated into policy and practice with the French Revolution, paradoxically both caused great destruction and laid part of the groundwork for preservation. Progressivism was taken partly to mean that the newly-produced is inherently superior to the old, but at the same time the rationalistic impulse to catalog and classify was one of the bases of systematic collections. Fortunately, the urge toward empathy with the past that emerged with the Romantics tended to balance the progressivist belief in the sole virtue of the new.

THE CONCEPT OF CULTURAL PROPERTY

One strong element of the Romantic movement was the attempt to feel the past, in part through intimate contact with old or significant objects or places. At its silliest the Romantic spirit led to a distorted, purely nostalgic view, and sometimes even to the creation of colorful pasts out of almost whole cloth. But it also brought to the study of history, for example, much broader sensitivity to what the past was really like than had existed in the more clinical approach represented by Gibbon. Above all, the Romantic spirit brought a conviction that the preservation of beautiful or historic objects was a responsibility of civilized man.

The Romantic movement also produced paradoxes: while the noblest expressions of cultural property's value, such as Goethe's, assert its importance to all of mankind, the actual manifestations of concern were (and indeed are yet) often fiercely nationalistic. Indeed, Peter Quennell has called nationalism essentially a product of the Romantic movement.[12] Perhaps the most visible example of nationalistic contention about the custody of cultural property, about which serious debate continues to this day, is the elements of the Parthenon frieze in the British Museum commonly called—at least in the English-speaking world—the Elgin Marbles. Not only does the debate involve questions of ownership and preservation, but Byron attempted to assuage what he construed as England's guilt in acquiring them by disclaiming the perpetrator on nationalistic grounds. In "The Curse of Minerva" he wrote:

> Daughter of Jove! In Britain's injured name,
> A true-born Briton may the deed disclaim,
> Frown not on England, England owns him not;
> Athena! No—the plunderer was a Scot.[13]

The Romantic spirit, by widening the acceptance of all human activity and creativity, also helped to lay the groundwork for the dissolution of a relatively unified Western culture, which is the hallmark of the Modernist era that began with the twentieth century. The fragmentation and diversity of our era have led to realization that both the past (including its tangible remains) and other cultures can contribute to the depth and richness of our human experience. Out of this realization has come a passion to preserve.

Some elements of cyclical attitudes toward preservation of the past, echoing perhaps the sequence of Renaissance historicism, Reformation iconoclasm, Enlightenment rationalism, and Romantic historicism, might be discerned again. Specifically, during the first half of this century, progressivist movements in design and the visual arts, such as the Bauhaus and the Machine Age esthetic, discouraged concern with the old. Desire for the new continued to some extent through the period of technological innovation and economic recovery and growth following World War II.

But growing consciousness of the opportunities presented by diversity, as well as of a new situation in human affairs, a new and absolute meaning of total war, have provided a major impulse toward our present concern with preservation of the past. H. L. White, for example, Commonwealth National Librarian and Archival Authority, said in 1956:

In Australia . . . it was the consciousness of the national effort involved in total war, as well as the threat which the emergency held for records themselves, which led the Commonwealth Government to establish an archival system in 1942. We should expect continuing crises provided by the discovery of atomic power to have a like effect on the preservation of archives in the future, unless we entirely abandon hope for our civilization. . . . In a very real sense the governmental and public attitude towards the preservation of archives is a measure of our faith in the future.[14]

The concept of cultural property, then, grew out of these changes in human consciousness and attitudes toward tangible products of the human spirit. The clearest enunciations of the importance of what we now call cultural property have been, not surprisingly, in response to threats of destruction through plunder and war. Although it was not until the nineteenth century that diplomacy brought about actual legal provisions, the idea of cultural property and the implications for its special status seem to have developed in the arena of international law.

Among early manifestations of concern for cultural property were Cicero's condemnation of the Roman proconsul Licinus Verres for plunder and destruction of works of art[15] and a bull of Pope Pius II in 1462 prohibiting destruction of the monuments of Rome. Although moral condemnation continued to develop during the Renaissance, in general destruction of art was seen as a terrible misfortune, but not as something that could be legally controlled. Similarly, during the Reformation the jurist Alberico Gentili discussed the issue of protection of art in his *De jure belli libri tres*, but he was still compelled to conclude that despoiling the conquered enemy of what we would now call cultural property was legal.[16]

It was not until 1690 that the interests of future generations appear first to have been cited as a basis for formal legal protection of cultural patrimony in time of war, this time by another Italian emigré named Justin Gentili.[17] Three generations later, in 1758, the Swiss jurist Emeric de Vattel stated the case for protection more explicitly:

For whatever cause a country is ravaged, we ought to spare those edifices which do honour to human society, and do not contribute to increase the enemy's strength,—such as temples, tombs, public buildings, and all works of remarkable beauty. What advantage is obtained by destroying them? It is declaring one's self an enemy to mankind, thus wantonly to deprive them of these monuments of art and models of taste. . . . We still detest those barbarians who destroyed so many wonders of art, when they overran the Roman empire.[18]

It was during the eighteenth century that public responsibility for cultural property was most tellingly manifested, through the founding of some of the most important public collections in the West. What is now the Bibliothèque Nationale opened to scholars in 1735, the British Museum opened in 1759, and the Archives Nationales in 1789; and the Louvre was founded in 1791. The same decree of the French revolutionary government that established the Louvre also "for the first time gave monuments a public status and nationalized private collections."[19] The extensive Napoleonic plunder, in which art was stolen for France rather than destroyed, was an affirmation of the importance of cultural property. Goethe, perhaps echoing Vattel, said in 1799 that "works of art are the property of mankind and ownership carries with it the obligation to preserve them. He who neglects this duty and directly or indirectly contributes to their damage or ruin invites the reproach of barbarism and will be punished with the contempt of all educated people, now and in future ages."[20]

Following the destruction of World War I, the Russian artist, poet, and visionary Nicholas Roerich launched a personal crusade for an international accord on the protection of cultural property. Roerich's efforts drew widespread attention to the need for improved protection, and a convention on the Protection of National Artistic and Historic Patrimonies, based on his proposals, was drafted for the Committee on Intellectual Cooperation of the League of Nations. Due to the onset of World War II, the Roerich Pact, as it came to be known, was never adopted worldwide, but a version was adopted by the American nations in 1935, and it was the basis of later international agreements.[21]

By 1945, once again in the aftermath of a great war, the idea of universal responsibility for the protection of cultural property was formally suggested. In the broad context of advancing the dignity of man through promotion of justice, liberty, and peace, the constitution of the United Nations Educational, Scientific and Cultural Organization (Unesco) has as one of its purposes to "maintain, increase and diffuse knowledge by assuring the conservation and protection of the world's inheritance of books, works of art and monuments of history and science."[22]

It is in the area of cultural property law that paradoxes about the conservation of the world's cultural patrimony are thrown into highest relief. The loftiest justifications, such as Goethe's, for the special protection of cultural property derive from the assertion that such property is important to, and at least in a broad sense belongs to, the entire human race, both present and future. "Life is short, art long," Hippocrates said, and the political boundaries of the world also have had relatively short lives in the long sweep of history.

Sharon Williams, a legal scholar specializing in cultural property law, takes the stance that international traffic in cultural property promotes intercultural understanding and the advancement of mankind:

> Nationalism has led states to attempt to divide up a civilization's work. This is evidenced by the value laid on great works of art. . . . They add prestige to national and state art galleries. The question is posed, however, whether the state which has become the "owner" of such a work has exclusive rights attached to it? States are responsible to not only their own citizens but on a broader plane to the civilization of which they form an integral part. Thus a state has a dual role to play. It is accountable to lessen nationalistic fervour and to promote cultural interchange between nations, which is necessary as a means of promoting peace and harmony.[23]

It is also sometimes argued that cultural property can be better cared for physically in a state other than the one of its origin. The better condition of the elements of the Parthenon friezes in the British Museum than those in place on the Parthenon itself is indisputable, although the legitimacy of their residence far from their rightful context continues to be disputed.

Yet nationalist considerations remain primary, and "cultural exploitation" must be taken into account. An obvious point is the staggering flow of works from nations rich in art or cultural objects, to those that are economically wealthier but perhaps poorer in artistic or other cultural resources. At least as important is that the removal of objects or fragments from archaeological sites means the loss of scientific archaeological evidence. This activity is thus a major cause of damage and destruction, regardless of any larger philosophical questions of rightful ownership. Profit is usually the motive for such depredations, but as it is often difficult to sell the plunder in the country of origin, effective control of traffic across national boundaries becomes a major need. And as the commercial value of cultural property escalates, so does the incentive to plunder and smuggle.

The legitimacy of claims of national cultures should not be underestimated. Nevertheless, the common heritage of mankind theory has adherents. This viewpoint is well represented by Williams in her comparative study of legal protection:

> From the doctrinal point of view it is submitted that the common heritage of mankind theory constitutes a good foundation for the development of rules of international law in this area. This new trend in thinking, which thankfully moves away from the strictly nationalistic approach, may well constitute the ground upon which the whole protection system may take root.[24]

The 1978 Unesco *Recommendation for the Protection of Movable Cultural Property* also states the common heritage theory explicitly: "Movable cultural property representing the different cultures forms part of the common heritage of mankind and . . . every State is therefore morally responsible to the international community as a whole for its safeguarding."[25] This formulation recognizes, however, a major practical problem: even if it were somehow established that cultural property legally belonged to the entire human race rather than to any person, institution, or state, the agencies necessary actually to carry out protection and conservation reside in (and indeed are often agencies of) individual states.

Manfred Lachs, a judge on the International Court of Justice in the Hague, also recognized this paradox in 1984:

Thus it is [the Convention for the Protection of Cultural Property in the Event of Armed Conflict] which, for the first time, uses the legal notion of common heritage of mankind in the domain of culture—embodied in so many forms. That great historian Jacob Burckhardt once claimed that culture and state were entirely different phenomena, and culture must not be submitted to power—he saw in their link an evil, an evil to be avoided. But obviously it is threatened. Who can protect culture if not the state? It is the power of the state which has to yield to culture, by protecting it. That is the great importance of the Convention of 1954, which extends the boundaries of culture into the domain of international relations, and brings the notion of the "cultural heritage of all mankind" into the legal dictionary which, with the passage of time, has been enriched by other concepts of common heritage: outer space and the ocean floor. This, I think, is Unesco's great achievement on which I wish to congratulate it: it has made culture a legal notion.[26]

The seabed and outer space are clearly extra-national, so any protective measures for them are necessarily formulated internationally. It is interesting to note that universal responsibility for immovable cultural property and the environment are linked in the 1972 Convention for the Protection of the World Cultural and Natural Heritage. The transition from expressions of concern and proposals for legal protection to actual laws, treaties, and pacts has been a long one, but the pace of protective measures that are at least in principle binding seems to be growing.

The art historian Irving Sandler has said: "A work of art is not just a piece of property like a chair or table. At least, it ought to possess the status of a dog or a cat. We have laws prohibiting cruelty to animals. We ought to have laws prohibiting cruelty to works of art."[27] In fact there is a significant body of legal protection for cultural property, although we do not yet have an artistic humane society that Cullen Davis's neighbors could have called when he smashed his "ancient Chinese art." In much of this law, libraries and archives and their collections are on a par with works of art, monuments, and archaeological remains.

The subject of cultural property law is a large and complex one, as Lyndell V. Prott and P. J. O'Keefe's projected five volumes on the subject suggest. Only enough will be offered here to suggest the relationship between libraries and the larger universe of cultural property. It may be useful first to say a few words about mechanisms of protection, especially about international recommendations and conventions.

Much of international law is customary; that is, it is based on norms that have evolved over the centuries. The validity, and especially the enforceability, of customary international law are much debated, but it is nonetheless the basis for much of what does work in the relations among nations. The more tangible basis of international law is agreements actually formulated among nations: treaties, pacts, and conventions. These instruments may be compared with contracts, in that following development by two or more states, they undergo formal procedures by each state to assert adherence to the provisions of the instrument.

Prott and O'Keefe identify a third force in international law, a product of the twentieth century: international organizations such as the United Nations, Unesco, and the International Court of Justice, to which states have ceded lesser or greater amounts of authority to produce international law.[28] Among international organizations it is, of course, the work of Unesco that is particularly relevant to our present interests, and specifically we are interested in Unesco recommendations and Unesco-sponsored conventions.

Conventions are multinational agreements that have the force of international law, with both the strengths and limitations that implies. However, formal ratification by signatory nations involves legislative action by each of those nations, which may require adjustments in domestic laws. Thus, despite limitations of international enforceability, conventions may have a tangible impact on the matter at hand.

Unesco recommendations may also appropriately be subsumed under the heading of international law. Prott and O'Keefe claim that Unesco recommendations represent

a kind of benchmark . . . of accepted principles and standards on the subject they deal with, [and] they are often followed by national lawmakers and thus become part of the general principles of law recognized by civilized nations. (By general consent the word "civilized" is now regarded as unnecessary.) UNESCO Recommendations are, therefore, not to be ignored: they constitute a significant body of legal principle and UNESCO members have an obligation to seriously consider them, where possible implement them, and to report on the measures they have taken in regard to them.[29]

Furthermore, the recommendations are a basis upon which conventions may be negotiated; the 1970 Convention on the Means of Prohibiting and Preventing the Illicit Import, Export and Transfer of Ownership of Cultural Property grew out of a 1964 Unesco recommendation of similar title.

The legal protection of archaeological sites, buildings, and monuments, and the closely related area of control of traffic in cultural property across national boundaries, are almost wholly outside the scope of this study, but collectively represent the largest body of cultural property law. Although there are other motives involved, these laws represent a major case of societal intervention in the preservation of cultural property. While not all of the formal legal protections are wholly relevant to libraries, and despite variable effectiveness in actual practice, this growing body of national and international laws demonstrates broadening public concern with the protection of cultural property.

Earlier in history any enemy property, with the partial exception of religious edifices, had been fair game for destruction, plunder, spoliation, and vandalism in time of war. Efforts to limit such assaults, earlier almost wholly moral rather than legal, have been described. The first actual codification of the idea that cultural patrimony should be acceptable neither as normal military objective nor as spoils of war was in the Lieber Code of 1863. The code was unilateral; it was formulated for the United States War Department by the lawyer Francis Lieber and adopted for the conduct of United States troops in the field. The code provided that "classical works of art, libraries, scientific collections, or precious instruments . . . as well as hospitals . . . should be secured against all avoidable injury, even when they are contained in fortified places whilst besieged or bombarded."[30] This code is particularly significant because all later provisions for the protection of cultural property during armed conflict grew from those included in it.

Under the initiative of Alexander II of Russia, an attempt was made at an international conference in Brussels in 1874 to compile a code of conduct for war on land. The code included, for the first time on the international level, provisions for protection of cultural property. The declaration of the Brussels conference was never ratified, but these early efforts came to fruition in the first codifications of international law, the products of the Hague Peace Conferences of 1899 and 1907. Included among a total of seventeen conventions on the conduct of war are provisions for the protection of cultural property.

In an effort to strengthen protection for cultural property, the International Museums Office drafted an international Convention for the Protection of Historic Buildings and Works of Art in Time of War, which was based on the work of Nicholas Roerich. The draft was submitted to the League of Nations in 1938, but the outbreak of war in 1939 prevented its adoption. It had, however, been adopted in 1935 by a number of western hemisphere states.

The devastation of cultural property in two world wars made horrifyingly evident how inadequate the Hague Conventions were. After World War II, Unesco set up a Museums and Monuments Division, which developed the International Convention for the Protection of Cultural Property in the Event of Armed Conflict, signed at the Hague in 1954. By 1985, seventy-three countries had acceded to or accepted the Convention.[31] It is this 1954 Hague Convention, the first comprehensive international agreement for the protection of cultural property, that is the primary current international law on the subject.

It is not appropriate to go into detail here on the provisions of the various conventions for the protection of cultural property during armed conflict. In general terms, these instruments, each of which builds upon and expands its predecessors, provide for:

- Refraining from any hostilities directed against such property except in the case of military necessity [note the proviso, which was inserted for political acceptability]
- Making preparations for safeguarding prior to armed conflict
- Avoiding use of areas of cultural property for purposes that are likely to expose it to damage or destruction in the event of armed conflict
- Introducing by each state into its military regulations procedures for the protection of cultural property, including prohibition of vandalism and plunder
- Providing for a category of cultural property of the greatest significance that is entitled to special protection ("immunity")
- Refraining from moving cultural property out of occupied countries or restitution if it has been carried away (especially restitution of archives, which are considered to appertain to their territory of origin).

The flow of artistic and historic objects, including books and manuscripts, from colonies to the imperial powers, and from poorer to richer (although not always culturally richer) nations, along with the growth of scientific archaeology, has been the impetus for national laws from as early as the fifteenth century, but such legislation started in earnest late in the nineteenth century. Such laws in their most comprehensive form include provisions about the control of archaeological digs, official scheduling of culture property, and control of sale, export, or import. National laws providing for official inventories or schedules of cultural property will be mentioned later, and the control of digs and of traffic are outside the scope of this study. They nevertheless must be acknowledged collectively as a major sphere of national and international intervention in the protection of cultural property.

Although the United States does not have export laws, it does have a series of laws, dating from 1906, protecting certain archaeological sites. Among the more far-reaching United States cultural property laws is the National Historic Preservation Act of 1966, which established the National Register of Historic Places. All in all the United States, in part because it has been one of the major importers of cultural property, and in part because of its strong noninterventionist tradition in general, has had much less governmental involvement in cultural property legislation than many other countries.[32] There is, however, a significant body of state and local historic preservation law in the United States.

The most typical provisions of national laws regulating traffic are either flat prohibitions of export of cultural property, or export control and licensing systems. In order to make such policies effective, however, responsibility must also be placed on receiving nations to control importation of cultural property that has been exported in violation of the laws of the country of origin. Thus international agreements are necessary for curbing the illegal flow of works of art and artifacts.

The major international agreement in this area is the 1970 Convention on the Means of Prohibiting and Preventing the Illicit Import, Export and Transfer of Ownership of Cultural Property. This provides, among other things, that parties to the convention agree to set up mechanisms for issuance of export certificates for cultural property that can legally be exported, and that they agree to direct their own customs officers to require such certificates on incoming material. Subscribing states must encourage their museums, libraries, and archives, as cultural institutions, to insure that their collections are built up in accordance with universally recognized moral principles.[33]

Regardless of any philosophical stances one may take about the universality of cultural property, and despite obvious difficulties in enforcement, laws controlling international traffic in cultural property currently seem to be the best approach to the two aims of curbing cultural imperialism and reducing profit-motivated vandalism of sites and monuments. They also represent, in part, another major instance of societal intervention in the protection of cultural property.

There are two other categories of cultural property law aimed at conservation of the integrity of historic and artistic objects. One of these is the legislation in some countries that involves the state in the actual preservation of important cultural property, including that owned by private institutions or by individuals. The other is moral right laws, which intend (among other things) to preserve the integrity of a creator's work.[34] A number of Unesco recommendations and Unesco-sponsored conventions assert the responsibility of nations for the protection and conservation of cultural property within their jurisdictions; the most comprehensive Unesco recommendation will be discussed below.

National cultural property laws often include schemes for inventorying and classifying the nation's patrimony, usually both movable and immovable, as defined by some measure of age or significance or both. In some countries, all protected cultural property is the property of the state. The law of some countries also includes provisions for conservation, in addition to registration procedures.

France and Italy have perhaps the most extensive such legislation. It provides for, among other things, state intervention in the preservation of highly important cultural property if the private or institutional owner has not done so. If the owner cannot pay for the necessary conservation work, the state may assist, but may either try to recoup the cost from the owner or, in extreme cases, expropriate the property.[35] One can only assume that such provisions are invoked rarely if at all, but they are among the clearest and most telling statements of societal responsibility for conservation of cultural property.

In Hungary we have some indication of how extensive state intervention in the care of books and manuscripts actually works. "Historic materials held by private individuals and corporate bodies [most often churches] are regarded as part of Hungary's common cultural heritage." Under this doctrine, all books, manuscripts, and maps meeting certain criteria of age or relevance to Hungary must be declared to the Hungarian National Library, in part so that they are accessible through listing in the national bibliography. Such documents, or collections of documents, are considered "protected." Among other things, the owner is obliged to keep the books in "suitable condition," and "if the owner cannot ensure the integrity and proper care of a protected document, the National Library can order its deposit in a state library." In turn, the Ministry of Culture has established two positions at the National Library for conservators exclusively to restore important items held in church collections. The Deputy Librarian concedes that while "these far-reaching regulations invest the National Library with the necessary authority to take steps to preserve historic library materials . . . there are no sanctions against persons who disregard the regulations . . . [and] the National Library rarely uses its power to enforce deposit."[36] This system is similar conceptually to those enacted in France, Italy, and many other countries, but it appears that the range of materials protected in the Hungarian law is considerably broader than the major national treasures envisioned in western European legislation. It is also based on genuine scarcity: Hungary's cultural heritage has undergone many vicissitudes over the centuries.

In many European countries, creators of works of art—whether visual, performing, musical, or literary—are deemed to have a moral right to claim, or in some cases disclaim, authorship (*droit de paternité*), and a right to the maintenance of their integrity (*droit au respect le l'oeuvre*), that transcend usual property rights. In the United States, however, the sole legally recognizable value has been economic, as reflected in copyright law and the law of contracts. In other words, in the United States the legal owner of the property (whether the property is tangible, as a sculpture, or intangible, as the intellectual property covered by copyright), has had total right of disposition of the property—including exploitation, alteration, or destruction—unless the creator or seller retained other rights by means of contract.

It must be emphasized that these author's moral right laws are concerned with protecting the interests of the creator in the integrity of cultural property, not necessarily the interests of the public. However, the author's *droit moral* is the basis for a growing body of legislation in the Untied States that recognizes public interest in the protection of cultural property. The impetus for these laws has come largely from acts of alteration or destruction of some highly visible works of public art, such as the cutting up (and thus effective destruction) of a sculpture by Isamu Noguchi in an office building lobby.[37]

The earliest such statute in the United States was the California Art Preservation Act of 1979, which for the first time outside the arena of armed conflict asserted statutory public interest in the preservation of cultural property. A related section of 1982 provides legal standing for organizations (in addition to the creator of the work) to protect creative works under certain circumstances.[38] While the actual applicability of this California statute is quite narrow, the law was a significant first step in codifying public interest in cultural property.

Other states are following suit. New York's 1984 Artist's Authorship Rights Act specifies only moral right and not public interest, but, unlike the California law, it also recognizes artist's multiples, and it includes—albeit under restrictive circumstances—neglect of works of art as a basis for action by artists.[39] More significant perhaps is the Massachusetts Moral Right Statute of 1985, which not only includes an assertion of public interest, but also extends broadly the types of creations covered. Prints, craft objects, and photographs are explicitly included. The Massachusetts law also covers destruction as actionable. Federal artists' rights legislation has been introduced by Senator Edward M. Kennedy, but it is restricted to painting, sculpture, and certain multiples; craft objects are not included.

These art preservation laws are intended primarily to prevent owners from drastically altering a living artist's intent by such acts as cutting works up to fit different spaces or painting a sculpture another color. They are of considerable theoretical interest to us as manifestations of legislated public interest in the protection of cultural property, and of creators' versus the public's rights in the conservation treatment of objects of artifact value.

The probability of invocation of moral right laws in the library area is, however, limited. The Massachusetts law could in theory be used by a book artist or craftsman (or by the state attorney general within fifty years after the death of the artist) to deter alteration of an artist's book "of recognized quality," for example. But the lower monetary value and relatively limited public visibility of books compared with paintings or public sculpture, and the costs of legal action, make actual suits unlikely. Moreover, because of the newness of this class of legislation, there are many potential questions yet to be worked out in case law. This legislation has, dismayingly, been controversial among conservators, some of whom are concerned that it might provide grounds for artists to sue over even conscientious and competent conservation treatments.

By far the most comprehensive legal, or at least quasi-legal, instrument on the conservation of cultural property is the 1978 Unesco Recommendation for the Protection of Movable Cultural Property. The recommendation, while it uses the phrase "museums and similar institutions," includes in its broad list of applicable cultural property books, manuscripts, documents, archives, maps, and photographs. Virtually all aspects of protection and conservation are covered in the recommendations, including relations between states and private owners of cultural property. Member states are urged to create inventories; provide appropriate security and environment; prepare for disaster; transport and exhibit objects protectively; educate the public about the importance (but not necessarily the monetary value) of cultural property; and provide means for conservation treatment services of the highest standard, including "a suitable system for training and the vetting of professional qualifications" of conservation personnel.[40]

LIBRARIES AND CULTURAL PROPERTY

The duality of books and manuscripts, which are both containers of explicit information and physical objects, was discussed earlier. All of the objects in a museum collection are normally considered cultural property, although this is not to say that all the objects are necessarily of equal importance or value. In a library, however, individual books or manuscripts may be valuable for their explicit information, as physical artifacts, or, very often, to some degree both. Research libraries as a whole, in their role as keepers of culture, must be considered cultural property—even if, as is most often the case, only a minority of individual items would by themselves be so considered.

In fact, research libraries face a dual challenge. The overarching circumstance is that they serve two purposes: meeting present reference, instructional, and research needs, and preserving culture, including cultural property, for the future. Their most obvious and immediate constituents—those who, one might say, pay the bills—are their current users, especially present students and faculty in the case of an academic research library. To the extent that research libraries have responsibility for preservation of culture, unknown users at an indefinite time in the future are the clients. Thus one of the major issues that research libraries must face, one that distinguishes them from other types of libraries, is allocation of resources between activities serving immediate needs and those serving long-range preservation. A more subtle and vexing subissue growing from this dual responsibility is allocating between present and future clients the finite, if often quite large, amount of use that items of artifact value, which in absolute terms are irreplaceable, can receive before becoming seriously deteriorated or even unusable.

There has begun to be some discussion of "the archaeology of the book," the exact study of the physical book that depends on relatively unaltered artifacts, and of the "museumization" of at least those books that are acknowledged to be rare. Both of these ideas affirm, knowingly or not, that at least portions of library collections are cultural property that must be carefully protected if they are to survive. But the library profession, and its clients, are so imbued with the principle of immediate service—indeed service is the first tenet of the American Library Association code of ethics—that the idea of further sequestering some classes of collections is repugnant, regardless of the long-term consequences of unrestricted or inadequately restricted use.[41]

In any case, because the artifact value of books falls on a continuum, lines of demarcation can only be arbitrary, and only a portion of the cultural property in libraries can realistically be sequestered from routine use. There is no obvious solution to the problem of protection for those items that are of potential or partial artifact value—value that will almost certainly grow with time. Surrogates of various types will certainly play a growing role.

Although thinkers concerned with cultural property as a whole have included libraries in the spectrum of cultural property for at least a century, library theorists largely have not. I have found in other work that writers on the theory and philosophy of librarianship, particularly those from the United States, have not recognized explicitly the relationship between research libraries and cultural property, and have barely recognized it even implicitly.

The commendable emphasis on service in the theory of librarianship, which as Jesse Shera points out grew out of the public library movement of the nineteenth century, has nevertheless obscured one of the central characteristics of research libraries.[42] While lip service is often given to preservation, the inescapable dimension that has been omitted from so much of the literature on the theory and philosophy of librarianship is time, and it is perhaps this element that most distinguishes research libraries from other types.

I have been speaking as if libraries have been ignoring preservation all this time, which of course is patently not the case. Preservation has in fact been a major concern of librarians from time immemorial. But, speaking of the United States at least, details of preservation were perhaps driven from the librarian's consciousness as being "sub-professional" in the aftermath of the Williamson report of 1923, which contributed so heavily to the professionalization of librarianship. Then, following what has been called the "long silence" about library preservation lasting from the 1930s into the 1960s, preservation became a major preoccupation of research librarianship.[43]

Nevertheless, the pressures to meet present needs is a growing problem, including (among other factors) the high costs of necessary automation and the alarming growth in both the rate of output of information and the unit cost of acquisitions at a rate far higher than that of the economy as a whole. At the same time the rate of deterioration grows. In order to help achieve an appropriate balance in the allocation of scarce resources between possibly vocal present and certainly silent future constituencies, it would seem useful to have a fuller and more coherent body of theory on research librarianship specifically, including its role in the universe of cultural property.

NOTES

1. G. Thomas Tanselle, "Bibliographers and the Library," *Library Trends* 25 (April 1977): 745-62.

2. David Gates with Nikki Finke Greenberg, "Mockingbird Lane's Born-Again Baron," *Newsweek* 17 Oct. 1983: 16-17. Wayne King, "Texas: State of Question Marks and Contradictions," *New York Times* 6 May 1984: A26.

3. Ralph Franklin,"Conjectures on Rarity," *Library Quarterly* 44 (Oct. 1974): 312.

4. Richard de Bury [Richard Aungerville], *The Philobiblon* (Berkeley: University of California Press, 1948) 41-45. On Petrarch see, for example, Leo Deuel, *Testaments of Time: The Search for Lost Manuscripts and Records* (New York: Knopf, 1965), chap. 1. Lyndel V. Prott and P. J. O'Keefe, *Law and the Cultural Heritage*, vol. 1, *Discovery and Excavations* (Abingdon, England: Professional Books, 1984) 37.

5. Paul Philippot, "Historic Preservation: Philosophy, Criteria, Guidelines," *Preservation and Conservation: Principles and Practices*, ed. Sharon Timmons (Washington, D.C.: Preservation Press, 1976) 367-82.

6. United Nations Educational Scientific and Cultural Organization, *Protection of Movable Cultural Property: Compendium of Laws* (Paris: 1984) 1:336.

7. Deuel, *Testaments of Time*, chap. 14. Ignacio Bernal, *Mexico before Cortez: Art, History, Legend* (New York: Doubleday, 1963).

8. C. V. Wedgwood, *The Sense of the Past: Thirteen Studies in the Theory and Practice of History* (New York: Collier, 1967) 36. (Originally published as *Truth and Opinion*, 1960.)

9. David Lowenthal and Marcus Binney, eds., *The Past before Us: Why Do We Save It?* (London: Temple Smith, 1981) 17.

10. Michael Hunter,"The Preconditions of Preservation: A Historical Perspective," *Our Past before Us: Why Do We Save It?*, eds. David Lowenthal and Marcus Binney (London: Temple Smith, 1981) 26.

11. See, for example, H. W. Janson, *History of Art* (New York: Abrams, 1977) 379-80; Ferdinand Schevill, *History of Florence* (New York: Harcourt, Brace, 1936) 417-18.

12. Peter Quennell, *Byron in Italy* (1941; New York: Viking Press, Compass Books, 1957), 257-58.
13. *The Works of Lord Byron* (Philadelphia: Lippincott, 1876) 2:448. Byron reiterated these sentiments in "Childe Harold's Pilgrimage" (*Works* 1:44-45).
14. H. L. White, foreword, *Modern Archives: Principles and Techniques*, by T. R. Schellenberg (1956; Chicago: University of Chicago Press, 1975) vii-viii.
15. Cicero *Against Verres* 2.
16. Alberico Gentili, *De jure belli libri tres* (Hanau, 1598), trans. John C. Rolfe of the edition of 1612 (Oxford: Clarendon Press, 1933) 310-14.
17. Stanislaw E. Nahlik, "La protection internationale des biens culturels en cas de conflit armé," Académie de Droit International, *Recueil des Cours*, part 1 (Leyden: A. W. Sijthoff, 1968) 74.
18. E. de Vattel, *The Law of Nations*, ed. Chitty (1844) 366ff., quoted in Sharon Williams, *The International and National Protection of Movable Cultural Property: A Comparative Study* (Dobbs Ferry, NY: Oceana Publications, 1978) 5-6.
19. Emil Alexandrov, *International Legal Protection of Cultural Property* ([Sofia?]: Sofia Press, 1979) 21.
20. Goethe in the *Propylaen* (1799), quoted in Julius Held, "Alteration and Mutilation of Works of Art," *The South Atlantic Quarterly* 62 (Winter 1963): 26.
21. Alexandrov, *International Legal Protection* 14-15.
22. Unesco, *Constitution of the United Nations Educational, Scientific and Cultural Organization* (1945), Art. 1.
23. Williams, *The International and National Protection of Movable Cultural Property* 53.
24. Williams, *The International and National Protection of Movable Property* 2.
25. Unesco, *Recommendation for the Protection of Movable Cultural Property*, Paris, 28 November 1978.
26. Manfred Lachs, "The Defences of Culture," *Museum* 147 (1985): 168.
27. Quoted in Douglas C. McGill, "U.S. Bill on Artists' Rights is Debated," *New York Times* 19 November 1986: C33.
28. Prott and O'Keefe, *Law and the Cultural Heritage* 1:71.
29. Prott and O'Keefe, *Law and the Cultural Heritage* 1:77.
30. *Code of War for the Government of the Armies of the United States in the Field* (1863), as quoted in Williams, *International and National Protection* 16.
31. Lachs, "Defences of Culture," *Museum* 147 (1985): 167.
32. Prott and O'Keefe, *Law and the Cultural Heritage* 1:63-65.
33. Unesco, *Compendium* 21-23.
34. In fact, moral right laws evolve from intellectual property (copyright, etc.) law rather than cultural property law.
35. Unesco, *Compendium* 123-29; Williams, *International and National Protection of Movable Cultural Property* 106-112.
36. Gedeon Borsa, "Preservation of Historic Library Materials in Hungary," *Library Conservation News* 15 (April 1987): 4-6.
37. Franklin Feldman and Stephen E. Weil, with Susan Duke Biederman, *Art Law: Rights and Liabilities of Creators and Collectors* (Boston: Little, Brown, 1986) 426ff.
38. Calif. Civil Code, sec. 989(b) (1).
39. New York Code, Arts and Cultural Affairs, sec. 14.
40. Unesco, *Compendium* 386-92.

41. "On Professional Ethics," *American Libraries* 12 (June 1981): 335.

42. Jesse H. Shera, "Librarianship, Philosophy, of," *ALA World Encyclopedia of Library and Information Services*, ed. Robert Wedgeworth (Chicago: American Library Association, 1980) 314–15.

43. William J. Crowe, "Verner W. Clapp as Opinion Leader and Change Agent in the Preservation of Library Materials," Ph.D. diss., School of Library and Information Science, Indiana University, 1986, 130. Crowe's terminus is the mid-1950s; I believe that within the library profession itself, the "silence" lasted well into the 1960s.

6

Scholarly Resources for the Study of the Third World: The Case of Africa

Mary Niles Maack

This paper presents a historical overview of scholarly communication in African studies, and examines the creation and dissemination of research on tropical Africa as it relates to libraries. The main chronological focus is on the four decades of library development since World War II; the geographical focus is on the accessibility of Africanist research in the United States and in Africa. However, because research in African studies is international in character, it is important to place its evolution within a global context. Philip Altbach, a social scientist known for his studies of publishing in developing countries, aptly characterizes the realm of scholarly activity as a world with no borders, where "the metropolitan centers of scholarship—largely in North America and Western Europe, and, to a lesser extent in Eastern Europe—dominate the rest of the world."[1] This center-periphery relationship is particularly apparent in African studies, where the flow of knowledge has historically been from north to south. Despite this imbalance in the flow of books and information, there has been a growing recognition of the interdependence among scholars from the industrialized countries and their colleagues in Africa.

The role of libraries in facilitating communication among Africanists is also being recognized as a critical issue that must be dealt with in an international context. A review of the literature on the role of Africana library collections in the United States and in Africa indicates that a double information gap exists. On the one hand, American scholars have limited access to research originating in Africa, due to the underdeveloped status of local publishing. Conversely, African scholars have limited access to materials issued abroad, due to the high cost of these publications and the inability of local libraries to procure scarce foreign exchange funds for such purchases. This paper attempts to explore the effect that the nature of available library resources has had on the growth of knowledge in Africa and about Africa.

THE SCHOLARLY STUDY OF AFRICA: A HISTORICAL OVERVIEW

Prior to the European exploration and colonization of Africa, great centers of Islamic scholarship existed in those regions where the Muslim religion had taken root. By the late nineteenth century, there were fine private libraries in major centers of learning like Timbuktu and Sankore. A small class of learned Muslims also existed in other parts of the western Sudan, and one Senegalese scholar has devoted a lengthy monograph to the study of Islamic literature produced in the Senegambia region.[2] Both foreign and locally produced manuscripts were available in African centers of the trans-Saharan trade, but the lack of printing restricted the broader communication of African Islamic scholarship.[3]

It was not until the period of European exploration that printed information on African culture, religion, and geography became accessible to scholars in the West. Although accounts of early Portuguese exploration of the African coast date back to the fifteenth century, scientific publications about the continent did not begin to appear until the eighteenth century. One of the earliest of these studies was the result of the historic mission by a young French botanist, Michel Adanson, who did extensive research in Senegal from 1745 to 1753. The great value of Adanson's contribution lay in his careful collection of specimens of tropical plants, which he took back to France. Unfortunately, his lack of access to the work of contemporary scientists led him to devise his own classification system. Because of this, his publications fell outside the mainstream of botany in Europe, where the Linnaean taxonomy was being adopted.[4]

Over the two centuries that followed Adanson's botanical mission, four distinct patterns of Africanist research evolved. The earliest approach was that of the research mission staffed by European scientists who, like Adanson, carefully collected data and specimens in Africa and then returned to Europe, where they completed their research and published their work. The second research pattern was the applied scientific study carried out by a trained specialist, who was often a colonial officer on the staff of a government agency. By World War I, technical experts such as engineers, cartographers, and doctors were employed by most colonial governments. A third pattern of research, that of carrying out and publishing basic research in Africa, began in 1937 with the establishment in French West Africa of the first multidisciplinary research institute. The creation of such institutes by France and by other colonial powers was in many instances the first attempt by colonial authorities to support fundamental research in Africa. In addition, the staff of the new research institutes often were the first to engage in a sustained effort to provide resident scientists with access to documentation—including books, journals, photographs, and recordings, as well as collections of specimens and ethnographic objects. Finally, after World War II, a fourth pattern of research emerged in Africa, that of scholarly studies carried out in African universities.

RESEARCH MISSIONS AND FOREIGN RESEARCHERS

During the two centuries since Western scientific study was first introduced in Africa, the majority of all scholarly monographs and articles on Africa have continued to be written by Western expatriates who came to the continent on missions that ranged from several months to many years. Even after the colonial governments began to employ a small contingent of resident scientists, they also supported studies done by outside experts.

There are numerous examples of research missions of this type sponsored by colonial authorities, or by other agencies or learned societies in France and Britain. Several of these missions were of major importance—such as the 15,000-kilometer study tour undertaken between 1908 and 1910 by Auguste Chevalier, a botanist from the Muséum National d'Histoire Naturelle, and the famous Dakar-Djibouti ethnographic mission, which was carried out from 1931 to 1933 under the auspices of the Musée de l'Homme. In both instances, specimens and other items collected on the tour were taken back to France, where they were analyzed and placed in museum collections. The work of British scholars who made field trips to Africa was sometimes sponsored by the Colonial Office or by learned societies, such as the Royal Geographical Society, which had made Africa its special concern since its foundation in 1830.

Other learned bodies, such as the Royal Anthropological Institute, also had an interest in Africa, and in 1926 a scholarly society devoted exclusively to Africa was established in Britain. This body, the International African Institute (IAI), has made a significant contribution to scholarly communication through its quarterly journal, *Africa*, and through its bibliographies. From 1932 to 1939, the IAI also sponsored Fellows, who carried out an impressive series of field studies with funding from the Rockefeller Foundation.[5] In 1944, an even more ambitious ethnographic survey was initiated by the IAI, and was subsequently published in over fifty volumes.

By the close of World War II, the work of scholars and scientists sent on missions from Europe often began to serve as a complement to that of local research institutes and scientific agencies. However, during the 1950s the pace of European Africanist research increased significantly. At the same time, African studies centers were being created in the United States, and American researchers became more numerous in Africa. As a result, the writings of foreigners continued to make up a significant portion of the published literature on Africa even after the advent of independence. A dramatic illustration of this situation is shown in Anthony Killick's bibliography on East African economies, which covers works published between 1963 and 1975. Of the 639 authors cited, only eighty-four, or 13 percent, were East Africans. Although an analysis of the entries by year shows a decreasing proportion of foreign authors, by 1975 Africans had only written one-quarter of the economic publications cited (twenty-three out of ninety-two).[6]

Although the increased employment of nationals in African universities and research institutes has drawn more Africans into the network of scholarly communication, their writings do not yet account for a majority of the research publications dealing with Africa. A number of political and economic factors have contributed to this anomaly. Political pressures and opportunities often led the first generation of highly trained Africans to be drafted into administration rather than remain in research. In more recent years, economic problems have limited the scholarly productivity of younger African scholars, who often work in institutions that lack adequate funding for laboratories or field work. This is frequently a problem in Senegal, where almost no field work funding has been available since the early 1970s. Even though Africanists in Europe and America have experienced a dwindling of research funds, they continue to enjoy much greater governmental and institutional support than their counterparts in Africa.

Those African scholars who have enough support to carry out significant research often have difficulty getting their work published in a timely fashion, due mainly to a lack of scholarly presses in Africa that regularly issue journals and monographs. The limited number of publications from Africa cited by foreign scholars was shown in a recent citation analysis of the twenty-two books that received the Herskovits Award, given by the African Studies Association for distinguished, original scholarship on Africa. Out of a total of 4,821 references found in those books that received the award between 1963 and 1985, only 22.4% of the works cited (1,082) were published in Africa, whereas 77.6% were published in Europe or America.[7]

APPLIED RESEARCH

Applied research has been carried out in Africa for over a century, but there have never been effective mechanisms for disseminating such studies. Although both colonial and independent African governments have issued numerous reports in fields such as public health, sanitation, agriculture, geology, meteorology, tropical medicine, and mining, these are seldom published in scholarly journals. Dr. E. B. Worthington, a

British zoologist who conducted a survey of scientific work in Africa, in 1938 commented on the "waste of research" that resulted from the fact that few colonial officers were willing to undertake the additional labor of preparing their reports for submission to scientific societies. He noted that the data gathered by scientists in Africa was generally published in annual departmental reports, bulletins, pamphlets, and occasional papers. Because such publications were administrative in nature, the findings published in them generally remained outside the normal channels of scholarly communication. Worthington was also concerned about the even greater inaccessibility of unpublished data gathered by medical, agricultural, and administrative officers. He remarked: "Some officers have collected notes of great scientific value about the people, their customs, food, diseases, etc. The bulk of these notes are kept in the files of the district offices where they are not easily unearthed [when needed] at a later date."[8]

In the introduction to his 1938 survey, Worthington commented that "a development based on a real understanding of Africa's potentialities has hardly yet begun, and will be impossible until the necessity of scientific research is recognized."[9] This recognition of the role science could play in development finally came in the decade following World War II, when the colonial powers allotted considerably more funding to applied research in Africa. During these years, which have been described as "by far the most active period in the history of colonial rule," a number of specialized research institutes were created by the colonial authorities.[10] When the work of this new generation of scientific establishments was reviewed by Worthington in 1958, he remarked that every subject had become far more specialized. He then concluded: "In Africa more science and development has been accomplished since 1938 than in the whole preceding period."[11]

By the 1950s several international bodies, such as Unesco and the Commission for Technical Cooperation in Africa, conducted surveys of scientific work and sponsored conferences to facilitate communication among scientists throughout Africa. From 1948 to 1956, over ninety inter-African meetings brought together researchers who discussed topics such as geology, meteorology, water, soils, wild life, animal diseases, health and medicine, housing, economics, labor, education, and prehistory.[12] Following the independence of the African countries, international organizations continued to sponsor scholarly meetings, and sometimes funded large-scale projects like the Unesco study of industrialization in Africa. In addition, new centers for training and research were created—such as the African Institute for Development and Planning set up in Dakar by the United Nations Economic Commission for Africa, and the United Nations Environmental Program, which has its headquarters in Nairobi.

Even though scientists doing applied research in Africa in the 1980s have numerous links through international scientific networks, their work often remains unpublished or is issued in the form of mimeographed reports that have very limited distribution. It is evident that the situation has greatly improved since Worthington did his first survey of scientific development fifty years ago. However, some of the problems he identified then regarding the dissemination of applied research still have not been resolved.

Another problem that has continued to affect agencies for applied research is the lack of access to relevant literature in the field. Small collections of books, reports, and journals are usually kept in the offices or laboratories of those government agencies involved in research. However, such collections tend to be painfully inadequate in scope and organization. For example, when a union list of the books belonging to specialized agencies in Dakar was compiled in 1932, it was found that together all ten collections had no more than 3,000 books.[13] Many of these libraries continued to exist, but apparently grew very little during the next twenty years. In 1954 when a survey was done, none of the collections that had been inventoried in 1932 contained more than a few thousand volumes.[14]

The situation was no better in the British colonies, where researchers who wished to submit their work to scholarly journals were often forced to write up their research during home leave, when they could consult libraries in institutions such as the Royal Botanical Gardens at Kew or the Imperial Forestry Institute at Oxford. The pattern of turning to British establishments for research training and documentation persisted in the postwar years, leading the Ghanaian scholar Samuel Kotei to comment in 1972: "The cumulative effect of these practices has been that today there are richer collections of both published and unpublished studies [on Africa] in British, American and European libraries than in Ghana."[15]

INSTITUTES FOR FUNDAMENTAL RESEARCH

The creation of multidisciplinary research centers marked an important step in the institutionalization of science in Africa. All of these centers maintained at least a small corps of full-time researchers, and in some instances they also set up the first adequately funded research library in the country. These institutes also published important monographs and journals devoted to fundamental research, and in many cases they can be credited with establishing the first scholarly presses in their respective regions. This was true in French West Africa, where the Institut Fondamental d'Afrique Noire (IFAN), founded in 1937, became the first publisher that regularly issued scientific monographs. Also in 1937, the colonial governments of Uganda and the two Rhodesias joined with a number of private firms to create the Rhodes-Livingston Institute, which published a journal and carried out numerous inquiries on social conditions in central Africa. In 1945, the Portuguese founded a similar institute, the Centro de Estudos da Guiné Portuguesa in Bissau; and by the late 1940s the French had created research institutes modeled on IFAN in French Equatorial Africa and in the Cameroon. Around the same time, the Belgians established the Institut pour la Recherche Scientifique en Afrique Centrale, and the British set up two regional institutes for the social sciences—the East African Institute for Social Research at Makerere, and the West African Institute of Social and Economic Research in Ibadan.[16]

During the transition to independence, most of these institutes came under the authority of the new governments. Although some institutes initially received substantial support from Europe or from American sources like the Rockefeller Foundation, by the end of the first decade of independence, most research centers had become largely dependent on African funding, and were therefore affected by the economic difficulties and political priorities of the new states. In Senegal, the degree to which IFAN funding was cut back was clearly reflected in its publishing program. From 1950 to 1959, fifty monographs were issued; from 1960 to 1969 that number had dropped to twenty-seven; and from 1970 to 1983 only nine appeared. In addition to curtailing the funds for publication, the financially beleaguered Senegalese government reduced its support for field studies and added university teaching responsibilities to the work load of the institute's scientific staff. IFAN's new status as a research institute attached to the University of Dakar also made it more vulnerable to the student protests that shook the university in 1968. Although the commitment to fundamental research was never abandoned, IFAN has felt increased pressures to move in the direction of applied research.

Similar tendencies elsewhere have been noted by David Court, a social scientist who has taught in East Africa for many years. Court comments that "the trend . . . has been the reorientation of social science from predominantly individual intellectual enterprise to the service of government." Despite these pressures, Court observes that African research centers have contributed to a new theoretical orientation in the social sciences which, in their inherited form, were seen as lacking relevance to Africa. East African scholars also criticized social science research as "part of a process of cultural imperialism" to the extent that it emphasized system maintenance and "modernization." Court continues:

The consequent initial task for East African scholarship is hence to seek an understanding of the way in which these imported frameworks have affected the definition of East African society and to seek ways of viewing social phenomena in the total social context in which they are embedded.[17]

Continuing theoretical work of this nature is linked to the future of African research institutes, which are often poised in a delicate balance between the demands of the government that ultimately controls their funding and the priorities of the universities to which they generally attached.

AFRICAN UNIVERSITIES AND SCHOLARLY COMMUNICATION

Higher education on the Western model is a relative newcomer to tropical Africa. Between the two world wars postsecondary training programs were established in Nigeria, Ghana, Senegal, the Sudan, and Uganda, but aside from Fourah Bay College in Sierra Leone, no African institution offered university degrees until after World War II. Initially tied to metropolitan institutions (such as London University, the University of Louvain in Belgium, or the Universities of Paris and Bordeaux in France), these institutions generally offered few courses with African content. By 1960 there were only six universities or university colleges in sub-Saharan Africa, and all of these were rapidly transformed into full-fledged universities at the time of independence. In the following decade, their adaptation to the African setting was often painful, and even respected institutions like the University of Dakar and the University of Nairobi have been closed during periods of political protest.

One of the main issues faced by the new African universities is how to reconcile conflicting expectations in regard to their proper role in development, their research mission, and their teaching responsibilities. Sociologist Edward Shils expresses this dilemma well: "One of the main problems is that so much is expected of universities in poor countries. Some of the expectations are unreasonable, requiring of universities what no university could deliver."[18] In an attempt to arrive at some consensus on this debate, the African Association of Universities held a workshop in 1973 to "formulate a new philosophy of . . . university education."[19] The first three roles identified by this workshop all concerned the university's research mission. These were:

a) Pursuit, promotion and dissemination of knowledge: with emphasis on practical knowledge, locally oriented.

b) Research: with an emphasis on research into local problems affecting the immediate community.

c) Provision of intellectual leadership: not only with the production of knowledge, but also its wide diffusion for meaningful programmes of economic and social development.[20]

Despite this strong statement on research and on the need to disseminate knowledge, many universities in Africa today must focus their efforts on teaching a rapidly growing student body.

As a result of these priorities, few African universities have been able to maintain viable presses. In a survey of scholarly publishing in the 1980s, Hans Zell notes that the Ghana Universities Press has produced a negligible number of books due in part to paper shortages, and that the press at the University of Sierra Leone has curtailed its production because of the country's chronic balance of payment problems. Even the oldest and largest university publisher in Africa, the University of Ibadan Press, has experienced a sharp drop in its title output, and a number of books announced several years ago have not been issued. Zell also describes the situation as bleak in East Africa, where the presses in Addis Ababa and Khartoum have published little. On the positive side, the University of Nairobi founded a new press in 1987, and presses in the Ivory Coast and Tanzania have become more active.[21] Although several of the presses discussed above are known for quality publications, many of the fifty universities in Africa are unable to publish research in any form other than mimeographed reports by academic departments or colleges.

The effectiveness of African universities as research institutions has been further limited by the lack of adequate libraries to provide the books and journals needed for scholars to keep up with developments in their field. Among those countries in sub-Saharan Africa that reported the size of their academic library collections for the 1986 edition of the *ALA World Encyclopedia*, only five countries (Zaire, Ethiopia, Sudan, Uganda, and Zimbabwe) indicated that their largest academic libraries held between 350,000 and 500,000 volumes. The largest university libraries in Liberia, Ghana, Kenya, Malawi, and Zambia held between 200,000 and 300,000 volumes; those in Burundi, Rwanda, Madagascar, and Sierra Leone claimed over 100,000 volumes. If the largest academic libraries in Nigeria, Senegal and South Africa were added to the list above,[22] one could estimate that there are now over two dozen university libraries with more than 100,000 volumes; this marks a significant accomplishment achieved in less than forty years. Nonetheless, among the remaining eighteen universities which did report on their holdings, library collections range from 80,000 volumes in the Congo to 15,000 in Niger and 14,000 in Chad.

Although statistics such as those cited above provide one indication of the poverty of African university libraries, they often fail to show how underdeveloped these libraries really are. On a 1981 study tour of African universities, the Ghanaian librarian Kwami Avafia attempted to gather information on the University of Angola Library, where the librarian had failed to return his questionnaire. He observed: "A visit to the university library revealed only a small collection at the central library, with even this on closed access, and no professional librarian was in attendance!"[23] With 75,000 volumes, this library would have ranked nineteenth among those African libraries reporting their collection size to the *ALA World Encyclopedia* in 1985.

While visiting libraries in fourteen African countries between 1983 and 1988, I also observed numerous instances where academic libraries were not functioning at a normal level. For example, the university library in Gabon was closed much of the time because the air conditioning did not work; since the library had been designed allowing for no natural ventilation, the small staff offices were often so hot that it was impossible to work. In Sierra Leone, frequent power outages meant that staff and readers had to work without adequate lighting, and in the Cameroon the university library had been in disarray for several years waiting to move into a new building that remained unfinished due to budget cuts.

Even where physical facilities are adequate, collection development is often a critical problem. A comparison of the figures submitted by African universities to the 1980 and 1986 editions of the *ALA World Encyclopedia* reveals that during that period almost no African university libraries grew by more than a few thousand volumes; one major exception is the University of Addis Ababa collection, which increased from 250,000 volumes to 500,000 volumes due to the assistance of the Ford Foundation and the United States government. Without external aid, many university libraries have a great deal of difficulty adding to their collections. Although funding varies greatly, budgets for most libraries are meager. A recent survey of the academic library budgets for the nine Francophone universities showed a range from approximately $200,000 at the Universities of Dakar and Abidjan to just over $13,000 at the National University of Benin, which had a collection of only 30,000 volumes.[24]

Certain universities in former British colonies are somewhat better endowed, such as the University of Khartoum library, which had a yearly budget of $400,000.[25] However, many of these countries have weak currencies and stringent restrictions on foreign exchange—a very serious situation when "as high as 90 percent of all library materials are purchased outside the continent."[26] While certain countries, such as Zimbabwe, have allotted some of their scarce foreign exchange funds to the university library, purchases of all library materials have been severely curtailed in many African states. Even in a comparatively prosperous country like Nigeria, in 1988 two major academic libraries were described as "operating under extremely difficult constraints that have prevented them from acquiring the basic sources essential for them to continue being first rate institutions."[27] Growing concern over the impact of this "book famine" has also been voiced by historian Michael Crowder, who worries that the education offered "at universities like Ibadan and Makerere, at one time as good as one could get in Europe or America, is falling back to the standard of rural junior colleges in the southern United States before the Second World War."[28]

The unfortunate situation at these two universities is not unique at a time of economic crisis, when many African libraries are unable to keep pace with the growing volume of scholarly literature published in Europe and America. Hans Zell noted in 1987:

> foreign exchange is so scarce that many university and public libraries have not been able to purchase books in the past two or three years, much less maintain current periodical collections. Most bookshops present a picture of empty shelves . . . and scholars are divorced from the material to pursue their studies, to maintain their understanding of developments taking place in their disciplines elsewhere in the world and to keep their teaching and research up to date.[29]

The effect that this situation has had on African scholarship was described by a Kenyan researcher who observed that he was embarrassed to find European and American colleagues at international meetings citing recent research on Kenya that he had not seen because it was not available anywhere in the country. The curtailment of library acquisitions is especially critical in Africa because most scholars there simply can not afford to import books at their own expense. Crowder noted in 1986 that "a book at £10 sterling would in Uganda cost a lecturer at Makerere the equivalent of his month's salary." He comments:

> The ultimate consequence of all this is that Africa is in serious danger of falling as far behind Europe in terms of scientific and technological education as it was at the time of the European occupation in the nineteenth century. The starry sixties when the young African universities seemed to be joining the international academic community on equal terms have given way to our current decade of despair where African universities slip faster and faster behind their European and American counterparts.[30]

AFRICAN STUDIES AND AFRICANA COLLECTIONS IN THE UNITED STATES

At the time that full-fledged universities were being established in Africa, a few American universities began to create African studies centers in order to foster interdisciplinary study. The founding of the first centers, at Northwestern University in 1948 and at Boston University in 1953, must be seen in the context of a general postwar expansion of graduate work in international studies. The number of Ph.D.s produced annually in international area studies increased from approximately 100 in 1948 to 225 in 1951, and then rose to nearly 1,000 by 1970.[31] By this time, area studies had developed considerably, and African studies centers had been set up at thirteen major research universities: five located in the East (Boston, Columbia, Cornell, Princeton, and Yale); six in the Midwest (Chicago, Indiana, Michigan State, Northwestern, Notre Dame, and Wisconsin); and two in California, the University of California at Los Angeles (UCLA) and Stanford. During this period when African studies were expanding in the United States, the parallel development of the first research universities in Africa seemed to mark the opening of an era of scholarly communication among African and foreign researchers.

THE GROWTH OF AFRICANIST LIBRARY RESOURCES

To keep pace with the growing need for research materials produced in and about Africa, the libraries at nine American universities had employed an African studies bibliographer by 1970, and a few, such as Northwestern, had specialist catalogers as well. All of these major university libraries had previously acquired a certain amount of Africana to support faculty research, but Northwestern, under the influence of anthropologist Melville Herskovits, was the first institution that aggressively expanded its collection. With additional support from a $40,000 Ford Foundation grant, the library was able to acquire approximately 1,500 volumes a year during the 1950s. Under the Farmington Plan (1948–1972), in which responsibility for acquiring foreign materials of research interest was divided among major American research libraries, Northwestern agreed to acquire publications from all African countries south of the Sahara, except for the Union of South Africa. This assignment did not provide extra funding, but it allowed the library to obtain certain materials, especially European Africanist publications, through Farmington agents.

The Farmington Plan offered no help with the problem of acquiring materials from Africa, so Northwestern librarian David Jolly attempted to increase acquisitions by "indoctrinating" all scholars going into the field "with the need to pick up copies of local publications as they came across them." Although he described the results of these efforts as "meager for the most part," he remained convinced of "the importance of on-the-spot collecting in the African territories," and urged that specialist bibliographers undertake cooperative acquisitions trips on behalf of a number of libraries.[32] Buying trips, some of them cooperative in nature, were undertaken by librarians from several of the universities with major African studies programs, such as Yale, Indiana, Michigan State, and UCLA. These trips were often discussed at meetings of the library committee of the African Studies Association (ASA), which was one of the first three committees set up by the ASA when it was founded in 1957.

The *African Studies Bulletin* has occasionally featured reports on library resources, and in a 1967 ASA survey of African studies programs, the size of Africana collections was given for those libraries that maintained such statistics. At that time, Yale had 12,000 volumes; Wisconsin 15,000; UCLA 16,000; and Boston 18,000. However, with two full-time librarians and a collection of more than 30,000 volumes, 300 periodicals dealing with Africa, and 30 African newspapers, Northwestern remained preeminent in the field.[33] In 1971 this collection had grown to 50,000 volumes and by 1984/85 its size had more than doubled, reaching an estimated 124,000 volumes.[34]

SCHOLARLY RESOURCES FOR THE STUDY OF THE THIRD WORLD

Despite the apparent success of Northwestern's efforts to collect widely in Africa, the curator, Hans Panofsky, remained skeptical of attaining truly comprehensive coverage. He observed in 1965 that "in spite of the enormous efforts spent by so many institutions on the acquisition of Africana, perhaps only slightly more than half of the material issued in Africa ever reaches an American library."[35] Among the serious gaps identified by Panofsky are proceedings of inter-African conferences, legislative proceedings of national governments, local government documentation, and documentation pertaining to voluntary organizations. Panofsky's concerns are echoed by Peter Duignan, the compiler of an extensive guide to African resources available in American libraries. In 1969 he attributed the "weak and scattered" nature of African collections to the late growth of interest in African studies and to the fact that these collections had been built "spasmodically and without much planning."[36] As a result of his survey, Duignan believed that although both current and retrospective monographs on Africa that were published in Europe were well represented, materials generated in Africa were "seriously underrepresented." He also emphasized that adequate library resources were concentrated at only a few universities.

The unequal distribution of resources has proved to be an issue of continuing concern to the ASA. In a 1964 survey of Africanists who had been elected fellows of the ASA on the basis of their academic achievements, it was shown that only 12.9 percent were affiliated with one of the recognized African studies centers, whereas 19 percent were "the only representative of African interests at their own institution."[37] With the decline of federal funds and foundation grants for language and area studies, African studies centers have grown little. Twenty years after the 1964 survey of ASA fellows, the compilers of the guide to American library resources on Africa commented that the evolution of doctoral research on Africa, combined with a depressed academic job market, has led an increasing number of serious research-oriented Africanists to seek employment at small colleges. They further note that "the product of this development is 'the lonely Africanist,' the researcher who is denied ready access to Africana resources in the United States."[38]

Although the lack of direct access to African publications will remain a problem for many Africanists, access to resources available though interlibrary loan has improved markedly during the past decade. This improvement is due to the fact that most of the strongest Africana collections are housed in libraries that subscribe to one of the major library utilities, OCLC (Online Computer Library Center) or RLIN (Research Libraries Information Network). Any other library that has access to these library networks can also use their extensive bibliographic databases for verification and location of titles held by these specialized collections. Furthermore, those libraries subscribing to the interlibrary loan module of either OCLC or RLIN can obtain items more quickly by placing their requests electronically. Another major benefit available through the RLIN database is the capability of doing sophisticated searches using full Library of Congress Subject Headings or key terms in a relevant title. These subject searches can be further defined by country of publication, language, or year of publication. Although this kind of search is expensive, it can serve to locate items in ways that were extremely difficult if not impossible with manual systems. For example, a scholar could easily retrieve works published in Russian on political affairs in Angola, scan titles on Senegalese politics that were published in Senegal, or obtain a printout of all 190 cataloged works in the Shona language.

In August 1987, I conducted a series of searches on the RLIN database in order to determine the extent to which RLIN can provide scholars with subject access to materials from and about Africa. For each of the fifty countries in sub-Saharan Africa, a search was done using truncated subject headings in which the name of country was the first element in the subject phrase. This search technique yielded a combined total of 39,680 postings reflecting RLIN's fully catalogued holdings on individual countries. In addition, a search with the word "Africa" as the beginning of a subject phrase retrieved 20,149 postings. It should, however, be emphasized that this does not represent all relevant items on Africa that have been catalogued in the database. For example, any entries on Nigeria that did not begin with "Nigeria" or "Nigerian" could not be retrieved by this method.

A customized search was also commissioned by Robert Hayes of UCLA in order to obtain comprehensive data on African language materials that were catalogued by RLIN libraries and loaded into the database as of August 10, 1987. The most numerous African language holdings were in Afrikaans, with 4,860 postings. Next came Swahili with 1,024 postings, followed by Niger-Kordafanian with 360, Shona with 190, Hausa with 187, and Southern Sotho with 105. Other African languages represented by 60 to 100 postings included, in descending order, Yoruba, Zulu, Xhosa, and Somali. It must be stressed that these records do not represent the total holdings of those libraries that are members of RLIN. What percentage of any one library's collection is included depends on the extent to which manual card catalog records have been converted to electronic form, on when the last tapes were loaded in the system, and on what the library's policy is in regard to the level of cataloging given to particular categories of publications. For example, the Northwestern University library, which participates in RLIN, has loaded one tape into the system that covers cataloging from 1970 to 1982. It was estimated that 63,000 Africana titles were in this batch, but 18,000 were given brief cataloging with no subject headings. Access through RLIN to Africana materials will be greatly expanded when Northwestern tapes are available for materials cataloged since 1982, and for records converted from 30,000 manually produced cards.

In addition to the library network databases, Africanists can also tap into to other databases available through vendors such as DIALOG or WILSONLINE, which offer fee-based online searching of many bibliographies and indexes. Through both of these vendors, the database known as LC-MARC (Library of Congress-Machine Readable Cataloging) can be searched for titles of books and journals catalogued since 1968. In addition to author, title, and subject searches, LC-MARC titles can be retrieved by language, geographic location, place of publication, name of a specific press, series title, or conference location. Furthermore, one or more of these elements can be correlated with year of publication. For example, a scholar could request a search for those books issued by the University of Ibadan press since 1980. Another important multidisciplinary database available online or on CD-ROM is *Dissertation Abstracts International*, which allows searchers quickly to identify theses on specific African countries, languages, or ethnic groups.

While no database now offered through DIALOG has Africa as its primary focus, in a 1984 dissertation John Howell used Morocco as a test case and found that twenty-three DIALOG databases contained more than 140 postings on that country. These included science databases such as Chemical Industry Notes, MEDLINE and GeoArchive, as well as databases in agriculture such as AGRICOLA and CAB Abstracts (Commonwealth Agricultural Bureaux), and major social science files such as PAIS (Public Affairs Information Service) International and Sociological Abstracts.[39] Although few of these databases index any publications from Africa, they do provide flexible access to materials issued in industrialized countries.

In the four decades that have passed since Northwestern created its African studies center, significant Africana collections have been built up in American universities, and scores of electronic databases with citations relevant to Africanists have become available. Although the crucial problem of acquiring research materials from Africa has not been resolved, the fact that the RLIN database alone provides subject phrase access to nearly 40,000 titles on specific African countries opens up existing resources in a way never before possible.

THE USE OF AFRICANIST RESOURCES: A CASE STUDY

The growth of Africana collections in the United States and the availability of online databases is easy to document, but the role of library resources, print and electronic, in the actual work of scholars is less apparent. To address this issue, in the summer of 1987 I carried out an assessment of information needs and library use among Africanist faculty at UCLA. About one quarter of the faculty who have done research in Africa cooperated in this survey. These faculty members are part of a community of over sixty Africanists who offer approximately one hundred courses dealing with all aspects of African life and culture. More Africanists at UCLA have expertise on Eastern Africa than on other regions, but as a group their research interests span the entire continent. Faculty members interviewed for this case study were selected to represent the needs of Africanist researchers in a wide range of disciplines, and included professors from anthropology, architecture and urban planning, art history, ethnomusicology, geography, history, law, linguistics, political science, pediatrics, and public health.

Although these Africanist faculty members identified certain areas where the UCLA library could be strengthened, they were generally very pleased with the materials and services available. This can be attributed in part to the breadth and depth of the UCLA library collections, which contain six million volumes. Of these, there are approximately 100,000 volumes that deal directly with Africa; and there is an annual budget of $100,000 for books and periodicals in African studies. The employment of a full-time African studies bibliographer has also been very important in the development and use of this collection. One scholar commented: "I have not had much difficulty getting anything. If we do not have something, the bibliographer can often suggest where it might be borrowed." All of the Africanists surveyed were aware of the interlibrary loan service, but most of them indicated that they rarely request materials from elsewhere.

The use of the UCLA libraries by Africanists is largely influenced by the fact that they personally subscribe to or purchase many journals, books, and documents they consider relevant to their work. One scholar in art history regularly spends between $3,000 and $4,000 per year on books, and a political scientist remarked that he devotes $2,600 to serial subscriptions and another $2,000 to books. All respondents noted that they regularly buy publications while in the field, and some have had the good fortune to acquire existing collections related to their research. Even though they own relatively extensive personal collections, the majority of respondents indicated that they either use the library or send their research assistants to get materials for them about once a week. Many interviewees were quite enthusiastic about ORION, UCLA's online catalog, which now contains approximately 25,000 subject headings related to African countries.

Despite the strength of the library, it cannot provide all the research materials needed by Africanists—due in part to the great difficulty in acquiring material from Africa. Respondents were all quite aware of this situation; a law professor, for example, remarked: "You can't do serious Africanist research without going to Africa regularly." The difficulty of gaining access to materials from Africa was also mentioned by an anthropologist, who commented: "I am very concerned about getting publications from third world countries. . . . In the past I have been frustrated by not finding African publications. Perhaps I don't try hard enough." Several respondents noted that they have had difficulty obtaining reports of research institutes and university departments. This type of publication, which is usually mimeographed or printed in small editions, was cited as very important by faculty in virtually every discipline. Research papers from African universities that contain original, primary data gathered in the field are of great interest to scholars, but even at the doctoral level such studies are difficult to obtain. Both geographers and linguists also noted that student research papers at a masters level or below can be a valuable source of linguistic transcriptions and of place-specific information that may not be available in published materials.

Government publications were described as important by UCLA scholars working in medicine and science as well as in the social sciences. Statistical sources were considered especially valuable, as were historical collections of colonial documents and national development plans. Publications of nongovernmental organizations (such as trade unions, political parties, religious organizations, and professional associations) were also cited as providing useful social and economic information. These publications tend to be even more difficult to acquire than government documents, since there is no centralized source where one can purchase materials issued by different organizations.

Among other African materials that are not easily accessible at UCLA, local newspapers were most frequently mentioned. In 1988 the library subscribed to only eighteen dailies from nine African countries; thus there was no newspaper available on campus for four-fifths of the African countries. Weeklies, news digests, and British Broadcasting Corporation transcripts provide current information, but are not considered an adequate replacement for local newspapers. African periodicals are also considered important, but a frequent complaint voiced by Africanists concerns the irregular nature of journal publication in Africa. For example, the issue received in January 1989 of the major scholarly journal from francophone Africa, the *Bulletin de l'IFAN*, was dated July–October 1983. Similar problems were mentioned in relation to journals from Nigeria, Ghana, Tanzania, and Zambia.

Even though most respondents emphasized the need to personally acquire journals and other local publications while in Africa, their regular use of the UCLA library indicates that its collections do support many of their research needs. The kind of use Africanists make of the library naturally varies a great deal between different disciplines. However, one of the most common themes emerging from these interviews was the importance of interdisciplinary research in virtually all fields. Professors in ethnomusicology and pediatrics both stressed that it is essential for doctoral students to become completely immersed in the history and culture of the people they propose to study; a law professor noted that most of his secondary source material on customary law came from anthropological studies. Frequent use of historical materials was also stressed. Back issues of journals, colonial reports, missionary publications, and older monographs are used by researchers in fields as diverse as African ecology, anthropology, linguistics, geography, and ethnomusicology.

Use of subject bibliographies was also mentioned frequently. The majority of Africanists surveyed consult separately published, specialized bibliographies in addition to references from monographs and journal articles. Respondents also mentioned their use of current bibliographies appearing in the journals of their discipline, but they seldom referred to more general Africanist bibliographies, such as the *International African Bibliography, Africa Bibliography*, or the *African Book Publishing Record*. Only a few mentioned discipline-oriented tools such as a *Biological Abstracts*, the *Zoological Record, Sociological Abstracts*, and *Social Science Citation Index*. Among those faculty actively using online bibliographic tools were an anthropologist, who makes extensive use of POPULATION BIBLIOGRAPHY and SOCIAL SCISEARCH, and a pediatrician who has had MEDLINE searches done by the library. A geographer also has requested several online searches at the library, but could not identify the databases used. In the humanities, an art historian has had searches done of the online inventory of the National Museum of African Art. Most other faculty members did not seem to be familiar with the bibliographic databases now available in their fields, although they noted that their graduate students in fields such as urban planning and geography have had searches done.

Even though online resources have not been widely embraced by Africanists, a few faculty members in the survey had projects underway to download online information to create customized bibliographies. Others were using word processing programs or related software to enter bibliographic citations or manipulate research data, such as population or agricultural statistics, textual information from field notes, or lexical material on African languages. Two other UCLA Africanists were experimenting with videodisc and laserdisc technology that would enable them to incorporate both textual and visual information in a customized database. In one project, Questal software was being used to inventory the collections of the Museum of Cultural History; eventually the inventory will integrate information on the nature, style, and cultural origin of the artifact, with color photographs of the object stored on videodisc. In a second project, a geographer was transferring East African slides to a videodisc, which will be programmed so that viewers can study a sequence of images on specific themes such as ecology, peoples and culture, or deforestation.

Although the assessment on one campus reveals that Africanists may not yet be taking advantage of the full potential of electronic databases, they are certainly entering an era when recent innovations in computer software and laserdisc technology are opening up many new possibilities for storing and manipulating data. However, the heavy use of traditional library resources is likely to remain important, and travel to the field to gather both primary and secondary source materials will continue to be essential.

CONCLUSION AND EPILOGUE: THE CRISIS IN AFRICAN STUDIES

The pattern of library use by Africanists at UCLA demonstrates the value of a broad general collection as well as the importance of a strong Africana collection built up through book-buying trips made over the years. As a result of their historical development since World War II, other libraries at American universities with African studies centers also offer Africanists a wide range of materials. Six of the seventeen largest Africana collections surveyed in 1984 were in universities whose total library holdings were well in excess of two million volumes.[40] Furthermore, for those libraries where statistics have been reported, the size of the collection devoted exclusively to Africa ranged from 124,000 at Northwestern to 18,000 volumes at the University of Washington. When these figures are contrasted with the size of libraries in Africa, it becomes apparent that the largest American collections of Africana have more volumes than the entire collection of the largest university library in many African countries. The disparity is even more dramatic when one considers that Yale University library, with over eight million volumes, contains more than four times as many books as the total holdings of all the academic libraries in Nigeria.[41]

The seriousness of this widening knowledge gap between scholars in information-rich nations and those in the information-poor countries in Africa has led James Currey, a British publisher, to comment on "the danger . . . that African Studies books are retreating to the library shelves of the universities of the rich world."[42] Yet even in the United States, where sophisticated electronic access to information has been transforming scholarship, the situation is not entirely positive.

At a 1985 colloquium on African studies held at the British Library, an American librarian, David Easterbrook, remarked that the tremendous growth of Africana collections in the United States during the 1950s and 1960s was followed by the budget cuts, retrenchment, and inflation of the 1970s. However, he suggested that these problems had given way "to a cautious optimism for the 1980s encouraged by the continued expansion of individual and interinstitutional cooperation."[43] British participants attending the colloquium were much less sanguine. Patricia Larby, editor of the proceedings, offered the following summary:

Almost without exception the speakers . . . painted a gloomy picture of the immediate future against a background of shrinking budgets, staff losses and lack of research funding. . . . As a consequence scholars were relying increasingly on publications to keep abreast of developments in Africa instead of first hand knowledge acquired by personal visits, and as libraries were reducing coverage of research materials . . . this was not a state of affairs which could be acceptable to reputable scholarship.[44]

Although libraries in Britain and the United States struggle for funds to acquire materials needed for Africanist research, the wealth of resources on Africa available to them through cooperative networks is enormous when compared to the accessibility of such materials in African libraries.

The historical development of African libraries is too recent to allow for collection depth, and reduced funding has caused significant gaps in even the best collections. Hans Zell, who describes the present situation in Africa as a "book famine," is skeptical that this damage can be reversed through the use of CD-ROM or other computer-based resources. Zell feels that far from entering the electronic age, "most libraries in Africa are not 'on-line' to the technological advances and new opportunities; they are, on the contrary, very much *off*-line altogether to anything—to basic printed resources, let alone the new technology."[45] Although a few African libraries have launched automation projects, the majority are simply struggling to obtain foreign exchange funds to purchase scholarly materials that must be imported from abroad.

Over the past decade, the lack of funds for book purchases in Africa has also had serious implications for Africanist publishing in Europe and the United States. Currey notes that during the first 25 years after independence, "a substantial amount of scholarly work . . . appeared in print largely because there was a big enough market in Africa to make it worthwhile to run extra copies."[46] However, this pattern has changed drastically. Peter Warwick, an editor from Longman, the British publishing firm, pointed out that in 1975 his company could publish a revised Africanist dissertation in 2,000 copies and be able to count on sales in Africa for 25 percent of the hard cover edition; in addition, about 90 percent of the paperback reprint would also be sold in Africa. By 1980, only 1,250 copies of such a monograph would be printed, and only 10 percent of these would sold in Africa; furthermore a reprint in paperback would not be issued unless the work was assigned as a textbook. Five years later, Warwick noted that "such a project would not be viable without a firm US library sale or a subsidy."[47] By 1986, The Longman African division had been instructed "not to publish anything which is not demonstrably a university textbook."[48] Although the Longman academic division still issues a few monographs on Africa, one highly respected list, the Ibadan History Series, has been discontinued. Another casualty has been Heinemann's nonfiction publishing on Africa and the Caribbean.

28. Michael Crowder, "The Book Crisis: Africa's Other Famine," *African Research and Documentation* 41 (1986): 3.
29. Zell, "African Scholarly Publishing" 98.
30. Crowder, "Book Crisis" 5.
31. *Beyond Growth: The Next Stage in Language and Area Studies* (Washington, D.C.: Association of American Universities, 1984) 7.
32. David Jolly, "Northwestern University's African Program," ARL Farmington Plan Survey Docket" (1959) 6–7.
33. Norman R. Bennett, "African Studies in the United States," *African Studies Bulletin* 11 (April 1968): 86.
34. Jean E. Meah Gosebrink, *African Studies Information Resource Directory* (Oxford: Hans Zell, K. H. Saur, 1986) 253.
35. Hans E. Panofsky,"African Studies in American Libraries," *Library Quarterly* 35 (Oct. 1965): 301.
36. Peter Duignan, "Africana Collecting: A Slough of Despond," *Farmington Plan Newsletter* 30 (Oct. 1969): 36–37.
37. Panofsky, "African Studies" 300.
38. Corinne Nyquist and Leon P. Spencer, "The Lonely Africanist: A Guide to Selected U.S. Africana Libraries for Researchers," *ASA News* 17 (Oct. 1984): 2.
39. John Bruce Howell, "The Concept of 'Development Literature' and the Establishment of Criteria for a Development Database," Ph.D. diss., University of Illinois, 1984.
40. Nyquist, "Lonely Africanist" 5–16.
41. Figures from Nigeria are from the *ALA World Encyclopedia* 605.
42. James Currey, "The State of African Studies Publishing," *African Affairs* 85 (Oct. 1986): 609.
43. David Easterbrook, "International Library and Archival Cooperation: America," in *African Studies: Papers Presented at a Colloquium at the British Library, 7–9 January 1985*, ed. Lise Sternberg and Patricia Larby (London: British Library, in cooperation with SCOLMA, 1986) 153.
44. Patricia Larby, "Resources for African Studies: The Role of Libraries," *African Affairs* 84 (Oct. 1985): 607.
45. Hans Zell, "The Other Famine," *Libri* 37 (Dec. 1987): 294.
46. Currey, "African Studies Publishing" 609.
47. Warwick quoted by Michael Crowder, foreword, *African Bibliography—1985* (Manchester: Manchester University Press, 1985) xiii.
48. Currey, "African Studies Publishing" 610.
49. Abiola Irele, "An African Perspective on Publishing for African Studies," in *African Studies*, ed. Sternberg and Larby, 82.
50. Helen McLam, "'Food for Thought'—Relieving the African Book Famine," *Choice* 26 (July–August 1988): 1658.

Index

Academic librarians, 10; faculty status, 10–11, 28n. 6, 35n. 40; and the ideology of reading, 71–74, 82, 84; lacks power, 884; opinion of, 11; as scholars or librarians, 12; and subjects outside academe, 82

Academic libraries: acquisition policies, 17; administration of bureaucracy in, 80, 84; in Africa, 119–20, 129–31; ascendancy, 8–13; book expenditures, 14–15; collecting works by white males, 78, 81–82, 86n. 17; collection development, 8, 10, 12–17, 74, 75, 77–84; consumers of academic publications, 77, 83–84; directors, 11, 12; faculty influence on collection of, 10, 15, 79–84; faculty's opinion of, 84; funding, 9; heart of university, 1; history of, 5–8; and local public libraries, 20, 25; public use of, 43n. 91; rare book collections, 63–70; reflect versus create trends, 16; research value, nonrecognition of, 28n. 6; responsibilities of, 12–13, 71; scholarship role of, 71, 80; staff, 80; statistics on, 1. *See also* African studies; African studies centers

Academic library associations, 35n. 46

Acquisition policies, 17, 46, 52

Adams, Herbert Baxter, 20, 40n. 79

Adanson, Michel, 112

Advice to Young Men in their Conduct in Life (T. S. Arthur), 72

African Association of Universities, 118

African Institute for Development and Planning, 115

African Islamic scholarship, 112

African language materials, 124

African research centers, 116–18; funding, 117

African research missions, 113–14; and teaching, 118

African scholars: communication, 115; publications, 114–16, 131; at UCLA, 125–29

African scientific studies, written by westerns, 113–14

African studies: acquisition of, 122–23, 126–27; bibliographers, 122; case study in resources of, 125–29; centers in U.S., 113, 121–25; database searching, 124–25; funding, 115, 119–21, 123, 129–30; history, 112; interlibrary

loan, 123–124, 125; in libraries, 111–31, 121–22, 125–29; at New York Public Library, 23; printing and publishing of, 112, 114–17, 119, 129–31; at UCLA, 125–29
African Studies Association (ASA), 114, 122, 123, 131
African Studies Association of the United Kingdom, 131
African Studies Bulletin, 122
African Studies Colloquium, 129, 131
African universities, 118–21; libraries, 119–20, 129–31; poverty of, 119–21, 130–31; research funds, 114
Agassiz, Louis, 5
ALA World Encyclopedia, 119, 120, 132n.22
Aldrich, Richard, 42n.88
Alexander II, 101
Allocation of resources, for preservation, 106, 108
Altbach, Philip G., 111
American Academy of Arts and Sciences, 65
Americana collection, of P. Force, 47, 75
American Anthropological Society, 75
American Association of University Professors, 10
American Chemical Journal, 76
American Council of Learned Societies (ACLS), 56, 57
American Economic Association, 75
American folk song project, 58
American Geologist, 76
American Historical Association (AHA), 50, 57, 58, 75
American Historical Review, 76
American history collection, at Library of Congress, 47, 58
American Journal of Mathematics, 76
American Journal of Philology, 76
American Journal of Psychology, 76
American Journal of Sociology, 76
American Library Association (ALA), 11; code of ethics and rare book service, 107; hearings on Library of Congress, 48, 49; lobbied for H. Putnam, 49; proposed federal library bureau, 56; protests appointment of A. MacLeish, 57; Putnam seeks endorsement of LC's projects, 56–57
American Mathematical Society, 75
American Philosophical Society, 65
American Sociological Society, 75
American Statistical Association, 75
Ames, Fisher, 5
Anderson, Edwin H., 40n.83
Anglo-Saxon males, literature of, 78, 81, 86n.17
Annals of the American Academy of Political and Social Science, 76
Applied research, in Africa, 114–16, 117
Archaeological sites, removal of objects, 98, 102
"Archaeology of the book," 107
Archives Nationales, 97
Art works. *See* Cultural property
Artifact value of books, 107
Artist's Authorship Rights Act, 105
Artists: preserving integrity in work of, 103, 104; status of, 94
Association of American Universities, 11
Association of College and Reference Libraries, 35n.46
Association of College and Research Libraries (ACRL), 35n.46
Association of Research Libraries (ARL), 1, 24, 35n.46
Astor, John Jacob, 5
Astor Library, 5, 6, 20, 31n.18, 64
Athenaeum, 77
Atlantic, 77, 78
"Augmenting Materials for Research in American Libraries," 57
Australian archives, 96
Avafia, Kwami, 119
Axtell, James, 87n.24

Bacon, Sir Francis, 72
Bailyn, Bernard, 4

Bemis, Samuel, 53
Bender, Thomas, 3-4, 10
Beniger, James, 8
Bernal, Ignacio, 93
Bestor, Arthur, 38n.61, 50
Bibliographic control, 15-16; beginnings, 7-8, 33n.29; Library of Congress services for, 57, 58; New York Public Library, 33n.29
Bibliographic Society of America, 36n.46
Bibliographies, physical descriptions of items in, 90
Bibliothèque Nationale, 7, 12, 97; book catalog, 33n.29
Billings, John Shaw, 7, 21, 33n.29
Bodleian Library, Oxford University, 7
Book catalogs, 33n.29; at Library of Congress, 48
Book classification schemes, 16, 38n.61. *See also* Library of Congress
Book expenditure, 14-15
A Book for All Readers, 73
Book selection. *See* Collection development
Books Network for International Development and Education (BINDE), 131
Boston Athenaeum, 5, 6, 31n.18
Boston Public Library, 18; building for, 21; founding, 6; and H. Putnam, 49; print collection, 26; staff, 48
Boston University, Africana collection, 121
British Council, 131
British Museum Library, 7, 12, 97; book catalog, 33n.29; Spofford bases Library of Congress on, 47; staff, 48
Brodhead, Richard, 78, 81, 82
Brothers in Unity, 7
Brussels conference, on cultural property, 101
Bulletin of the New York Public Library, 24

Burckhardt, Jacob, 99
Byrd, Cecil, 68

A Calendar of Washington Manuscripts in the Library of Congress (H. Friedenwald), 51
California Art Preservation Act of 1979, 105
Card catalogs, 33n.29
Carlson, Chester, 22
Carnegie Corporation, 23, 56
Carnegie Library of Pittsburgh, 25
Catalog card service, Library of Congress, 33n.29, 50-51
Catalog of Books Represented by Library of Congress Printed Cards, 33n.29
Cather, Willa, 24
Catholics: burning of Protestants works, 94; as New York Public Library's trustees, 41n.86
Censorship: in collection development, 16-17, 18; of pro-German materials, 40n.84
Center for Research Libraries, 13
Centro de Estudos da Guiné Portuguesa, 117
Chairs system, at Library of Congress, 55-56
Chevalier, Auguste, 113
Chicago Public Library, 19
Childs, James B., 58
Chinese literature, acquired by Library of Congress, 53, 58
Choice of Books and Other Literary Pieces (F. Harrison), 72
Church libraries, 66
Cicero, 96
City University of New York, Graduate Center, 42n.91
Cleveland Public Library, 25
Cogswell, Joseph Green, 5, 6, 21
Cohen, I. Bernard, 2
Collection development, 8; academic libraries, 8, 10, 12-17, 74-75, 77-84; African studies, 121-31; based on publishers literary standards, 78; based on use, 16; cooperative ventures, 13, 25;

curriculum based, 78; excluding works not by white males, 81–82; faculty selections for, 10, 15, 74, 77, 79–84; financial support, 14–15; gifts for, 14–15, 37n.57; hinderance of collecting the best, 83; in history, 75; history of, 13–15, 37n.55; librarian's role, 84; Library of Congress, 46–49, 52, 75; New York Public Library, 21–25; non-collected materials lost for future, 82; in public libraries, 17–27; of radical materials, 22, 40n.83; research libraries, 75; for a universal research library, 12; of Western and classical literature, 15; works of Anglo-Saxon males, 78, 81, 86n.17

College of the City of Detroit, 43n.91

Colonial Africa, research in, 112–15, 117, 120

Colonial Office (British), 113

Columbia University, 20; student use of New York Public Library, 42n.91

Columbia University library: collection development, 37n.55; collection of radical materials, 40n.83

Columbia University School of Library Service, 2

Commission for Technical Cooperation in Africa, 115

Common heritage of mankind theory, 98–100

Confidentiality of readers, New York Public Library, 22, 40n.84

Consulting scholars, at Library of Congress, 55–56

Contract law, for artists, 104

Convention for the Protection of Cultural Property in the Event of Armed Conflict, 92–93, 99, 101–2

Convention for the Protection of Historic Buildings and Works of Art in Time of War, 101

Convention for the Protection of the World Cultural and Natural Heritage, 99

Convention on the Means of Prohibiting and Preventing the Illicity Import, Export and Transfer of Ownership of Cultural Property, 100, 103

Conventions on law, 101; and enforceability, 100

Coolidge, Elizabeth Sprague, 54

Cooperation, in collection development, 13, 25, 26

Cooperative Acquisitions Project for Wartime Publications, 13

Cooperative bibliographic projects, of public libraries, 26

Copyrighted material, at Library of Congress, 47

Copyright law, 104

Corporate collections, 65

Countryman, Gratia, 19

Court, David, 117

Cremin, Lawrence, 4

Critic, 77

Crowder, Michael, 120, 121

Cullen, Countee, 23

Cultural property, 91–108; books and manuscripts as, 91–108; definition, 92–93; destruction, 91, 93–97, 98, 105; impulses to collect and preserve, 93; international traffic, 98–102; laws to protect, 92–93, 96–106; and libraries, 104, 106–8; and nationalism, 95, 98; and the Reformation, 94, 96; and the Renaissance, 93–94, 96; residence of, 98; right to destroy, 91, 96; and war, 92, 96–97, 101–2

Currey, James, 129, 130

Curriculum: classical, 11; classical, and reading, 73–74; collection development coordination, 37n.55; library development based on, 78

Customary international law, 100

Dakar-Djibouti ethnographic mission, 113

Dana, James, 5

Danton, J. Periam, 14, 17

Darwin, Charles, 74, 75
Database searching, in African studies, 124–25, 128–29
Davis, Raymond C., 72
Davis, T. Cullen, 91, 99
Denver Public Library, 25
De Solla Price, Derek J., 2
Detroit Public Library, 20, 25, 43n.91
Deuel, Leo, 93
Dewey, Melvil, 48
Dewey's classification scheme, 16
DIALOG, 125
Dissertation Abstracts International, 125
Documents Division, Library of Congress, 58
Draper, Lyman, 65, 75
Droit moral, 105
Duignan, Peter, 123

East African Institute for Social Research, 117
Easterbrook, David, 129
Edelman, Hendrik, 14
Elgin Marbles, 95, 98
Eliot, Charles W., 9, 10
Emerson, Oliver Farrar, 77
Emerson, Ralph Waldo, 72, 73
Endowments, grants, etc., Library of Congress, 53–56
The Enlightenment, and cultural property, 94
Enoch Pratt Free Library, 20, 26, 43n.91
Erotica, and New York Public Library, 22
Espionage, and New York Public Library's policy on reading materials, 22
Ethnic research collections, at New York Public Library, 22–23
Ethnographic survey, of Africa, 113
Everett, Edward, 5, 6
Export of cultural property, 102–3

Facsimile representation, 90–91
Faculty: blind to library benefits, 83; influence on collection development, 10, 15, 74, 77, 79–84; as library directors, 11, 12; specialization of, 75
Faculty status, of librarians, 10–11, 28n.6, 35n.40
Fakes, books and manuscripts as, 91
Farmington Plan, 13, 58, 122
Federal library bureau, 56
Female authors, 81–82
Fields, James, 78
Folger Shakespeare Library, 64
Force, Peter, 47, 75
Ford Foundation, 122
Foreign language collections, at Library of Congress, 58
Foreign scholars, in Africa, 112–14
Foster, William, 73
Fourah Bay College, 118
Frederick Lewis Allen Room, at New York Public Library, 24
Free libraries, 6, 12
Free Library of Philadelphia, 26
Friedenwald, Herbert, 47–48, 51

Geiger, Roger, 9, 12
General Education Board, 56
Gentili, Alberico, 96
Gentili, Justin, 96
The Geography of Reading (L. R. Wilson), 15
Geological Society of America, 75
German publications, censorship of, 40n.84
German university libraries model, 5, 7, 9, 12, 14, 17, 21
Ghana Universities Press, 119
Gilman, Daniel Coit, 20, 75
GLanzraich, Gerri, 33n.30
Goethe, Johann Wolfgang von, 95, 97
Government depository libraries, 26, 44n.92
Government documents collection, standards for, 58
Governments, and public libraries, 18
Graduate programs, library materials for, 79

Graff, Gerald, 81
Graphic arts collection, at New York Public Library, 24
Gutenberg Bible, 54

Hague Peace Conferences, 101
Hanson, J.C.M., 57
Harris, Neil, 42n.90
Harrison, Frederick, 72
Harvard College, 5
Harvard University library, 9
Hastings, Charles H., 57
Hayes, Robert, 124
Hebraica, acquired by Library of Congress, 53
Heinemann (publisher), 130
Henry, Joseph, 46-47
Henry VIII, and manuscript destruction, 94
Herskovits Award, 114
Herskovits, Melville, 122
Higham, John, 3, 7-8
Historians, 3-4, 29n.9, 34n.38; at Library of Congress, 47-48
Historical societies, 65
Historical Society of Wisconsin, 65
History, collection development in, 75
Holley, Edward G., 7
Hosmer, James K., 19
Houghton Mifflin Literature Series, 78
Howell, William Dean, 77
Humanistic resources, collecting of, 13
Hungarian National Library, 104
Hungary, laws on cultural property, 104
Hunter, Michael, 94
Huntington, Archer, 54
Huntington Library, 64

Ibadan History Series, 130
Indica, acquired by Library of Congress, 53
Information scientists, 8, 33n.30
Institut Fondamental d'Afrique Noire (IFAN), 116, 117

Institut pour la Recherche Scientifique en Afrique Centrale, 117
Intellectual freedom, and collection development, 16
Intellectual life, libraries' role in, 3-4
Interlibrary loans, 13; of African studies, 123-24, 125; Library of Congress service, 50, 51, 57
International African Institute (IAI), 113, 131
International Court of Justice, 99, 100
International law, for cultural property, 92-93, 96-106
International Museums Office, 101
International organizations, and international law, 100
Irele, Abiola, 131
Islamic literature, 112

Jameson, J. Franklin, 55
Japanese literature, acquired by Library of Congress, 53, 58
Jefferson, Thomas, 6, 46
Jewish Division, at New York Public Library, 23, 24
Jewish Encyclopedia, 24
Jews, as New York Public Library's trustees, 41n.56
John Crerar Library, 19
The Johns Hopkins Studies in Historical and Political Science, 76
Johns Hopkins University, 43n.91; library, 20; Ph.D. graduates, 79
Jolly, David, 122
Journal of Political Economy, 76
Journals, published for scholarly communication, 76
Journals of the Continental Congress, 51
Joyce, William L., 63, 66

Kennedy, Edward M., 105
Keogh, Andrew, 40n.83
Killick, Anthony, 114
Kinkledey, Otto, 42n.88
Kotei, Samuel, 116
Kuhn, Thomas S., 2, 27n.4

Lachs, Manfred, 99

INDEX

Land grant colleges, 74
Larby, Patricia, 129-30
Lasswell, Harold, 17
LC-MARC (Library of Congress-Machine Readable Cataloging), 125
League of Nations, 101; Committee on Intellectual Cooperation, 97
Legal libraries, 66
Legislative libraries, 26
Lenox Library, 20, 64
Librarian of Congress: A. MacLeish, 45, 57; A. R. Spofford, 6, 19, 45-49, 72, 75; appointment of, 45, 46, 48; H. Putnam, 45, 49-59; J. R. Young, 48-49
Librarians. *See* Academic librarians
Library Bill of Rights (ALA), 16
Library buildings, 8; Library of Congress, 45, 47, 48, 55; New York Public Library, 20
Library-museum collections, 65
Library networks, regional, 26
Library of Congress, 45-59; acquisition policies, 46, 52; appropriations, 47, 53-54, 58; building, 45, 47, 48, 55; catalog card services, 33n.29, 50-51; cataloging and technical services, 46, 50, 57, 58; chairs system, 55-56; classification scheme, 50, 51, 57, 61n.38; collection development, 46-49, 52; copyright activities, 47; endowments, grants, etc., 53-56; extended access to, 48, 50; founding, 6; functions and roles, 46; interlibrary loan service, 50, 51, 57; Jefferson's library, 6, 46; list of accomplishments, 57-59; Manuscripts Division, 47-48, 50, 52-53, 58; microfilming, 53; Music Division, 54, 58; National Union Catalog, 13, 50, 56, 57; and the Panizzian model, 50; Peter Force collection, 47, 75; photoduplication service, 56; presidential papers, 52; publications of, 51; Rare Book Division, 65; Reorganization, 48; salaries, 55; scholars as employees, 54-56; service to libraries, 46, 48-52, 57, 58; staff, 46, 48
Library of Congress Mission to Europe, 58
Library of Congress Trust Fund Board, 54
Library science, in academic libraries, 80
Library suppliers, 33n.30
Library use: and collection development, 16; students and public libraries, 25, 42n.91
Lieber Code of 1863, 92-93, 101
Lieber, Francis, 101
Lincoln Center for the Performing Arts, 23
List of Maps of America in the Library of Congress (P. L. Phillips), 51
Literary establishment, Anglo-Saxon males as, 78, 81, 86n.17
Literary standards, of publishers, 78
Literature, academics as authority on, 78, 81
Local history collections, 26
Longman African division (publisher), 130
Los Angeles Public Library, 26
Louvre, 97
Lydenberg, Harry Miller, 21, 23, 24

McLachlan, James, 6
MacLeish, Archibald, 45, 57
McLuhan, Marshall, 90
Manuscript destruction, 94
Manuscript Division, Library of Congress, 47-48, 50, 52-53, 58
Martel, Charles, 57
Maryland Historical Society, 20
Massachusetts Institute of Technology library, 43n.91
Massachusetts Moral Right Statute of 1985, 105
Mathews, William, 72
Medical libraries, 7, 66
Medium, physical, of records, 89-91; description, 90; relationship to message, 89-90

Mencken, H. L., papers of, 26
Metropolitan Museum of Art, 24
Microfilming of archives, Library of Congress, 53
Middle East literature, acquired by Library of Congress, 58
Midwest Inter-Library Center, 13
Minneapolis Athenaeum, 49
Minneapolis Public Library, 19-20, 49
Moral right laws, 103-5, 109n.34; in library area, 105
Morgan Library, 64
Morrill Act of 1862, 6, 74
Mosher, Paul, 17
Mudge, Isadore, 13
Municipal reference libraries, 26
Musée de l'Homme, 113
Muséum National D'Histoire Naturelle, 113
"Museumization," of rare books, 107
Music Division, Library of Congress, 54, 58
Music Division, New York Public Library, 23, 42n.88
Muslim scholars, 112

National Archives, U.S., 53
National Historic Preservation Act of 1966, 102
Nationalism, and cultural property, 95, 98
National laws, cultural property protection, 103-6; in Hungary, 104; in United States, 105-6
National libraries: history of, 7; Library of Congress, 45-59; as universal research libraries, 12
National Library of Medicine, 7; *Index-Catalogue*, 7; *Index Medicus*, 7
National Program for Acquisitions and Cataloging (NPAC), 58
National Register of Historic Places, 102
National Review, 77
National Union Catalog, 13, 50, 56, 57
National University of Benin, 120

National Urban League, 23
Nelson, Alexander, 66
Nettlau collection, 40n.83
Newberry Library, 19, 64
New-York Historical Society, 65
New York Public Library: "alien enemies" on staff, 41n.44; Astor Library, 5, 6, 20, 31n.18, 64; building for, 20; collection development, 17-18, 21-25; collection of radical materials, 40n.83; consolidation of, 20; early bibliographic control, 33n.29; financial support, 25; government relationship, 18; graphic arts collection, 24; Jewish Division, 23; Lenox Library, 20, 64; Music Division, 42n.88; number of readers, 24; as Panizzian model, 21; performing arts collection, 23; publishing program, 24; research collection, 17-18, 25, 64; Slavonic Division, 23; student use of, 43n.91; The Research Libraries, 18; trustees, 18, 21, 22, 23, 41n.86
New York University, 20; student use of New York Public Library, 42n.91
Noguchi, Isamu, 105
Northwestern University, Africana collection, 121, 122-23, 124, 125, 129
Norwegian Library Association, 131

OCLC (Online Computer Library Center), 123-24
O'Connor, Thomas F., 14
O'Keefe, P. J., 99-100
The Organization of Knowledge in Modern America, 1860-1920, 3
Origin of Species (C. Darwin), 74, 75
Osburn, Charles B., 13

Panizzi, Antonio, 12, 21, 50
Panizzian model, 12, 14, 21, 50
Panofsky, Hans, 123
Parthenon friezes, 95, 98
Past, historical, recognition of, 93-95

Peabody Institute library, 20
Peer publications, collecting of, 75–79, 83–84
Performing arts collections, at New York Public Library, 23
Periodical indexes, 6–7; at New York Public Library, 33n.29
Periodicals, literary, 77, 86n.16
Perry, Bliss, 78
Personal collections, 64
Philippot, Paul, 92
Phillips, Philip Lee, 58
Physical description, of records, 90
Pisha, Louis, 37n.55
Pius II, Pope, 96
Political science, publications on, 76
Political Science Quarterly, 76
Poole, William F., 7, 19, 39n.76
Preservation, 16, 82
Preservation of cultural property: books and manuscripts of value, 91; and the Enlightenment, 94; impulses, 93; laws, 92–93, 96–106; in libraries, 106–8; and the Romantic movement, 94–95
Presidential papers, at Library of Congress, 52
Printing, in Africa, 112, 114, 119
Private libraries, 64–66
Progressivism, 9, 94, 95
Protection of National Artistic and Historic Patrimonies, 97
Protestant Reformation and cultural property, 94, 96
Prott, Lyndell V., 99–100
Public archival collection, 65
Public libraries: collecting local history materials, 19; collection development, 17–27; history of, 4, 6–7, 31n.18; local college cooperation, 25; and reading, 73; recreational reading collections, 42n.90; research collections, 25–26; student use of, 25, 42n.91. *See also specific names of libraries*
Public Libraries in the United States of America(U.S. Bureau of Education), 7

Public private collections, 64
Public use, of academic libraries, 43n.91
Publishers, literary standards of, 78
Publishing: of academics, 84; African, 112, 114–17, 119, 129–31; Library of Congress, 51; New York Public Library, 24
Putnam, Herbert, 45, 48, 49–59; at Minneapolis Public Library, 19

Quennell, Peter, 95
Quincy, J. P., 18–19

Radical materials, collecting of, 20, 40n.83
Rare book collections: in academic libraries, 63–70; history of, in academic libraries, 67–68; motives behind, 69; resist institutional handling, 63, 67, 69
Rare Book Division, Library of Congress, 65
Rare book libraries, 64
Rare book rooms, 70; create closeness with users, 69–70
Reading, ideology of, 71–84, 84n.2
Recommendation for the Protection of Movable Cultural Property (Unesco), 98–99, 106
Recommended reading, 73
Red Scare, 40n.83
Reference librarianship, 80
Renaissance, and cultural property, 93–94, 96
Research: in Africa, 112–13; and Library of Congress, 52; nonrecognition of libraries' value in, 28n.6; public library collections for, 17–26
Research libraries: in Africa, 116, 119–20, 129–31; collection development, 75; and cultural property, 104, 106–8; Library of Congress as, 45–48; statistics on, 1. *See also* Academic libraries
Research Libraries Group, 24
Research Libraries Information Network (RLIN), 123–25
Rhodes-Livingston Institute, 117

Ricci, David, 71, 81
Riverside Literature Series, 78, 86n.16
Robison, James, 91
Rockefeller Foundation, 56, 113
Roerich, Nicholas, 97, 101
Roerich Pact, 97
Romantic movement, 94–95
Rose, Ernestine, 23
Rowell, Joseph Cummings, 34n.38
Royal anthropological Institute, 113
Royal Geographical Society, 113
Rudolph, Frederick, 9
Russian literature, acquired by Library of Congress, 53, 58

Sandler, Irving, 99
Saturday Review, 77
Scholars: attracted by good libraries, 1, 37n.59; employed at Library of Congress, 47–48, 52, 55–56; influence on collection development, 14, 77; librarians as, 12; use of private libraries, 64–66; use of special collections, 67
Scholarship: libraries' role in, 2, 4, 7; and Library of Congress, 46–59; public library collections for, 17–26; and rare books, 63–70; resources for, in academic libraries, 5, 8–9
Schomberg, Arthur, 23
Schomberg Center for Research in Black Culture, 23, 42n.87
Science libraries, 5, 7
Scientific method of inquiry, 74–75
Scientific research: academic library resources for, 8–9; in Africa, 112–15; collection development for, 13–14; New York Public Library resources for, 22
Serial publications, African, 127
Sex hygiene, and New York Public Library, 22
Shera, Jesse, 107
Shiflett, Lee, 10–11
Shils, Edward, 8, 118
Showalter, Elaine, 81, 82

Slavonic Division, at New York Public Library, 23
Smithsonian Institution Library, 46–47
Social science research: in Africa, 117; collection development for, 13–14, 75
Society libraries, 5, 6–7, 31n.18
Sonneck, Oscar, 58
Sorge, F. A., 40n.83
Southworth, Mrs. E.D.E.N., 82
Special Libraries Association, 36n.46
Spofford, Ainsworth Rand: collecting Americana, 75; as Librarian of Congress, 6, 45, 46–49; on public library collections, 19; on reading, 72, 73, 82
Standards, of university presses and journals, 76
State universities, 6, 74
Students: required reading, 79; use of public libraries, 25, 42n.91
Studies in History, Economics and Public Law, 76
Study rooms: Library of Congress, 5; New York Public Library, 24

Tanselle, G. Thomas, 90
Tatum, G. Marvin, Jr., 14
"Temple of Science," 75, 80
Textbooks, reviewing of, 87n.24
Thompson, E. P., 82
Thwaites, Reuben Gold, 65, 75
Ticknor, George, 1, 5, 6
Tilden, Samuel J., 20
Tilden Trust, 20, 64
Trustees, of New York Public Library, 18, 21, 22, 23, 41n.86

U.S. Bureau of Education, 18
U.S. National Resources Committee, Science Committee, 15, 37n.59
U.S. Office of Education, 56
U.S. Office of Strategic Services, 36n.51
U.S. War Department, 101
Unesco. *See* United Nations Educational, Scientific and Cultural Organization

INDEX 145

Uniform cataloging standards, 57
Union catalogs, 13, 26, 50, 56, 57
Union List of Serials, 8
United Nations Economic Commission for Africa, 115
United Nations Educational, Scientific and Cultural Organization (Unesco), 97, 98–99, 100; Museums and Monuments Division, 101; on preservation of cultural property, 103; Recommendation for the Protection of Movable Cultural Property, 106; surveys of African Scientific work, 115
United Nations Environmental Program, 115
United States Army Surgeon-General's Library, 7
United States, cultural property legislation, 102–3, 105–6
United States South Seas Exploring Expedition, 5
Universal Jewish Encyclopedia, 24
Universal research library, 12, 17
Universities: ascendancy, 8–9; classical curriculum, 73–74; as multipurpose institution, 12; publications for information exchange, 76; rankings, and library facilities, 1; reputations made on basis of publications, 76; transformation, 8–9, 74–75. *See also* Academic libraries; African universities
University of Abidjan, 120
University of Angola Library, 119
University of California at Berkeley, 74; library, 17, 34n.38, 37n.57
University of California at Los Angeles, Africanist resources, 125–29
University of Chicago library, 19
University of Colorado, 2
University of Dakar, 117, 118, 120
University of Ibadan Press, 119
University of Illinois, 74; library, 14, 34n.38, 37n.55

University of Khartoum library, 120
University of Minnesota, 20
University of Nairobi, 118
University of Nairobi Press, 119
University of Sierra Leone Press, 119
University of Washington, 129
University of Wisconsin, 74
University presses, 76; in Africa, 119

Value, of books and manuscripts, 91
Vattel, Emeric de, 96
Verres, Licinus, 96
Vollbehr collection of incunabula, 54

Waples, Douglas, 17
War, and cultural property, 92, 96–97, 101–2
Warwick, Peter, 130
Wayne State University, 43n.91
Wedgwood, C. V., 93
Welch, William, 7
Wertheim Study, at New York Public Library, 24
West African Institute of Social and Economic Research, 117
White, H. L., 96
Whittall, Gertrude Clarke, 54
Widener Library, 64
Wilbur, James B., 53, 54
Williams, Sharon, 98
Willison, Ian, 4
Wilson, Louis Round, 15
Wilson, Woodrow, 77
WILSONLINE, 125
Wingspread Conference on New Directions in American Intellectual History, 3
Winsor, Justin, 19
Women librarians, 11
Works Progress Administration, 26
World library, Library of Congress as, 58
World War I: cultural property destruction, 97; and New York Public Library, 22
World War II, and collection development, 13, 36n.51
Worthington, Dr. E. B., 114–16

Xerography, 22

Yale University Corporation, and the Nettlau collection, 40n.83
Yale University library, 14, 36n.51, 40n.83, 43n.91, 129
Yarmolinsky, Avrahm, 23

Yehuda, Eliezer ben, 24
Yenawine, Wayne, 14
Young, John Russell, 48–49
Yudin, G. V., 53

Zell, Hans, 119, 121, 130

About the Contributors

PAUL N. BANKS is Associate Professor at the School of Library Service of Columbia University. From 1964 to 1981 he was Conservator and Head of Conservation at the Newberry Library in Chicago, and he has been in the forefront of the contemporary movement to preserve library materials.

JOHN Y. COLE is Director of the Center for the Book in the Library of Congress. He is the author of *For Congress and the Nation: A Chronological History of the Library of Congress*, and editor of *The Library of Congress in Perspective*.

PHYLLIS DAIN is Professor at the School of Library Service of Columbia University. She is the author of *The New York Public Library: A History of Its Founding and Early Years*, and co-editor of two *Library Trends* issues: "Libraries and Society: Research and Thought" (with Margaret F. Stieg) and "History of Library and Information Science Education" (with Donald G. Davis, Jr.).

NEIL HARRIS is Professor of History at the University of Chicago. He is the author of *The Artist in American Society: The Formative Years, 1790–1860* and *Humbug: The Art of P. T. Barnum*.

MARY NILES MAACK is Associate Professor at the Graduate School of Library and Information Science of the University of California at Los Angeles. She is the author of *Libraries in Senegal: Continuity and Change in an Emerging Nation* and has lectured and consulted widely in Africa.

WAYNE A. WIEGAND is Professor at the School of Library and Information Studies of the University of Wisconsin at Madison. He is the author of *The Politics of an Emerging Profession: The American Library Association, 1876–1917* and *"An Active Instrument for Propaganda": American Public Libraries During World War I*, and is editor of *Leaders in American Academic Librarianship, 1925–1975*.